Workplays

Workplays

Work and Career Play Scripts and Activities for Secondary Students

Second Edition

Hazel Edwards

Published in 2024 by Amba Press, Melbourne, Australia
www.ambapress.com.au

© Hazel Edwards 2024

All rights reserved. No part of this book may be reproduced or transmitted in any form or by any means, electronic or mechanical, including photocopying, recording or by any information storage and retrieval system, without prior permission in writing from the publisher.

Workplays was first published in 1984 by Longman Cheshire.

The play script 'Fire on Trial' was originally published in *Playing with Fire* by Hazel Edwards, published in 1989 by Thomas Nelson Australia.

This second edition was published in 2024.

Cover design – Tess McCabe
Proofreader – Megan Bryant

ISBN: 9781923116313 (pbk)
ISBN: 9781923116320 (ebk)

A catalogue record for this book is available from the National Library of Australia.

Contents

About the Author	vii
Introduction	1
Using Workplays	5
• How to Mock Up a Workplace	5
• Using Play Scripts	6
• Summary of the Group Approach	10
• Hints for Playmaking	10
• Checklist for Setting	11
• Getting Inside Your Characters	11
Hospital and Medical Areas	13
• Emergency	13
• Other Hospital/Medical Work	14
• Interviews	15
• A Day in the Life of …	16
• Work Flow Chart	18
• Play: Saturday Night Down in Emergency	19
• Activities: Suggested Play Scripts	30
Supermarket	33
• Mocking Up a Supermarket	33

- Interviews — 35
- Activities — 36
- Job Descriptions — 36
- Suggested Play Scripts — 43
- Fantasy: Talking to Trolleys — 46
- Writing a Group Story: Trolleypower — 50

Court — 53
- Procedure for a Day in Court — 53
- Interviews — 56
- Play: I Went to Court This Morning — 58
- Activities — 64

Emergency Services — 67
- Play: Fire on Trial — 67
- Video and Content Production — 74
- Content Production Notes — 75
- Checklist: Scriptwriting — 78
- Sample Storyboard — 79
- Shot Sizes — 81
- Activities — 83

Sports Centre — 85
- How One Group Worked — 86
- Interviews — 88
- Activities: Suggested Play Scripts — 91

Co-op — 93
- Play: Help Wanted — 94
- Activities — 98

Factory, Farm, Railway Station — 99
- Suggested Play Scripts — 100

Anywhere — 103
- Play: That's No Job for Them — 104
- Activities — 109

Co-working Spaces — 111
- Activities — 111

Self Employment — 113
- Working from Home — 113
- Activities — 117

Exploring Job Considerations — 119

About the Author

Hazel Edwards, OAM, is an award-winning author of books for children, teachers and adults.

An avid reader, as a young girl, Hazel Edwards wrote her first novel in grade six, a mystery about adventurous children stuck in a mine. This passion for writing continued after working in a secondary school and lecturing at teachers' college.

Aged twenty-seven, Hazel published her first novel, *General Store*, a book based on life in a rural town. It is Hazel's third published work that is her best known, the children's picture book classic, *There's a Hippopotamus on Our Roof Eating Cake*. This special imaginary friend has been cherished by children and parents alike and led to the dubious honour of Hazel being referred to as 'the Hippo Lady'.

Since its publication in 1980, the ageless *There's a Hippopotamus on Our Roof Eating Cake* has been reprinted annually, evolved into a series of seven picture books, inspired a junior chapter book, classroom play scripts, a musical stage production and a short movie. The Hippopotamus books have also been translated into Mandarin, Braille and Auslan signing for the hearing impaired and were presented as an official Australian Government gift to the children of Princess Mary of Denmark.

Whilst Hazel loves creating quirky, feisty characters for independent readers in her easy-to-read junior chapter books, she writes for all ages and has published over 220 books across a range of subjects and genres.

Published titles include *f2m:the boy within*, the first co-written young adult novel about gender transition and picture book *Stickybeak*.

Hazel has collaborated with experts to publish adult non-fiction titles such as such as *Difficult Personalities* (translated into seven languages), and helps people craft interesting memoirs and family histories in her popular workshops based on her book *Writing a Non-Boring Family History*. More recently a 'Complete Your Book in a Year' course has been offered via Zoom.

Awarded the Australian Antarctic Division Arts Fellowship (2001), Hazel travelled to Casey Station on the 'Polar Bird' ice-ship. This visit inspired a range of creative projects including the young adult eco-thriller *Antarctica's Frozen Chosen*, picture book *Antarctic Dad* and the memoir *Antarctic Writer on Ice*, as well as classroom playscripts.

A fan of interesting and unusual locations, Hazel has been a guest writer-in-residence in communities across Australia, a visiting author to Pasir Ridge International School in Indonesia and an author ambassador to Youfu West Street International School in China.

Passionate about literacy and creativity, Hazel has mentored gifted children and proudly held the title of Reading Ambassador for various organisations. Formerly a director on the Committee of Management of the Australian Society of Authors, Hazel was awarded an OAM for Literature in 2013. She is the patron of the Society of Women Writers (Vic) and in 2022 she was awarded the Monash University Distinguished Alumni Award for Education.

Introduction

To be 'on the job' is, of course, the best work experience. Apart from the particular tasks, some of the benefits are those of learning to get along with people of various ages and attitudes, following routines, coping with unfamiliar settings and talking together about work.

Work experience programs arranged by schools provide many of these opportunities but owing to organisational difficulties, limited time or placement problems, it is not possible to make these provisions for all students.

Alternative or supplementary work experience can be gained in the school itself by 'mocking up' work settings, finding out about actual jobs from the people who do them and playing the roles of workers in dramatised play scripts.

Workplays give students a chance to
- Gain some knowledge of a range of jobs
- Develop interview and research skills
- Identify temporarily with the viewpoints of unskilled and skilled, frustrated and satisfied, part-time and full-time workers

- Be aware of the layout and equipment associated with particular work settings
- Go out into the community and show initiative in discovering the requirements of various jobs.

These play scripts and suggested activities attempt to simulate the workplace. The aim is to give students a realistic idea of the types of jobs available and what each involves.

The suggested settings were chosen as workplaces where a range of occupations would be represented. Students may not have been aware, for instance, that hospitals employ plumbers, photographers or painters. Real nurses and doctors aren't like those portrayed in shows. The court was also chosen because many students know nothing about legal procedures nor about those involved in court.

After much trialling of the material, the suggestions of many students have been incorporated into the text and scripts.

The language has been simplified as much as possible so as to be within the range of all students. Those with reading difficulties might well make their contributions orally: they could interview workers, observe, and report back without having to write a great deal.

Some teachers might be daunted at first by the thought of the time required to set up a mock workplace in a regular classroom or in a corner of the gym. Then there is the additional task of convincing other teachers to co-operate with the making of props or even with changing rooms.

But these projects are worthwhile. Here are some of the advantages.
- The same work setting, such as the supermarket, can be used for several play scripts.
- Other subject-teachers and classes could be involved. The Graphics teacher and the Art class could design and make props. Perhaps the Woodwork class could also participate. If the school has a careers counsellor, that person will gain up-to-date local job information and will be able to share existing files on job requirements. Geography teachers could support the information-gathering exercises that the Workplays require.

- Various skills are called upon. The emphasis on observation and common sense rather than on formal reading/writing skills will enable all students to participate. Some will prefer to observe on the job and, for instance, make copies of typical background signs around the workplace, or watch the steps in a process and be able to replicate them. Others may read widely, interview or write out the actual script.
- Others again will be able to 'perform' without writing and reading scripts. Each can choose a job 'role' in the cast. By observing, asking questions of the worker and thinking about what the worker would be likely to do, the student can 'play' the role in the play.
- The final version could form the basis of a radio play or be a permanent record of the student's contribution in the class.

In summary, integrating plays and simulated workplace experiences in schools presents numerous advantages. While arranging on-the-job experiences for all students can be challenging, creating mock work settings within the school allows for essential skill development and a realistic understanding of the workforce. These projects offer a glimpse into various professions, fostering active participation and collaboration among students and teachers from different subjects. Despite logistical challenges, the benefits make these initiatives valuable in preparing students for the dynamic challenges of the professional world.

Using Workplays

How to Mock Up a Workplace

Possible workplaces are not, of course, limited to those mentioned in this book. One of the most relevant exercises is to simulate the workplace of the main local employer. If the Jelly Bean company down the road employs most of the people in your area, use it as the setting for your play scripts.

It is not necessary to reproduce every piece of machinery or furniture present in the original workplace and often props will be only approximate in shape. The important thing is that the students understand how the actual equipment operates. They need to know what the operator is required to do and what might go wrong if a mistake is made.

Labels can be very helpful. Students-workers may wear an identity card complete with photograph and occupation. Typical workplace signs such as 'Court 1', 'X-Ray Room', 'Deli' or 'No Smoking' can be drawn and attached to the wall.

Lists of factory rules, procedures, job requirements or codes of ethics can be mounted on the wall as an incentive for student discussion.

One group, using the Home Economics kitchen as a mock commercial kitchen, cooked the goods which they later served in the attached dining room, pretending it was a health food takeaway shop called 'Meals on Legs'.

It may be possible to produce and sell your 'goods' but check with school policy first. Anything which makes the work experience seem real will help the students.

Using Play Scripts

Play scripts offer a myriad of untapped opportunities for educators and schools. Here are a number of successful implementations and ideas from various educational settings, where the scripts serve as dynamic tools to break away from traditional teaching methods.

You can leverage them to introduce students to diverse professions, cultivate essential skills, and foster collaboration across subjects. Whether utilised for creating audio plays, video recordings, or live performances, play scripts provide a versatile platform for innovative learning.

1. **Choice of setting**
   After quickly flipping through the settings, it was decided to use a court of law. This was the workplace students knew least about. No-one had been inside a court.

2. **Background**
   They checked in the career centre for existing information about legal occupations and court procedures. Useful pamphlets such as 'What to do in court' and job descriptions of magistrate, barrister and clerk were found. They rang up the local magistrates court to find out when the court was sitting and if it was open to the public. Only the Children's Court was closed; the others opened at 10 a.m. so the group decided to pay a visit.

3. **Visit to the workplace**

   Students sat in the public seats at the back of the court and listened to a morning's cases. They sketched the layout and became familiar with people's titles and ways of addressing each other. Whilst working out the order of events, they also wrote down examples of legal phrasing to check later. During the lunch adjournment, when the staff weren't so busy, they asked questions and talked to the police waiting for traffic offences to be heard.

4. **Selection**

   Each student chose one occupation and agreed to go back and interview the appropriate person, the one who normally did that job. The group decided to make up a list of basic questions. Answers could be taped, written down or remembered.
   What do you do?
   What is your job called?
   What do you like/dislike about the work?
   Have you ever made any mistakes?
   How do you feel towards the accused?
   Do you think the sentences are fair?
   Can you remember any funny or unusual incidents? (This was to provide material for the students' plays.)

5. **'Mock-up'**

   A spare classroom was set up as a court. Furniture such as the magistrate's bench, witness box and bench clerk's microphone were improvised. The magistrate's stamp, various files, clock, Bible and coat of arms were borrowed, designed or simulated.

   The whole room became the court, as there was no need for audience space. Everyone was to participate. Those not speaking would sit in the public seats.

6. **Play script**

   Using the starting court script provided, students acted out the roles and decided on their own ending to the play. Then they discussed ways in which the play might be improved. Other characters could be added; the tension could be increased.

7. **Unresolved questions**

   During the discussion, certain unresolved questions arose which would have to be checked out by the students.
   - What were the most common cases? (They wanted to make their play representative of the type of cases frequently coming before the magistrate.)
   - Do more people plead guilty than not guilty, or vice versa?
   - Do people sentenced to prison go there immediately or can they return home first?
   - What are the average sentences for common offences?
   - What happens if you don't appear in court when summoned?
   - Why are more males than females charged?
   - What are the gender ratios of the magistrates? More males? If so, why?

8. **Brainstorming**

   Using the information gathered, together with any of the play script suggestions, students were invited to improvise their own plays with a court setting. Groups of 6–8 students were a workable size. One group designed a before and after court segment, enacting the crime, the sentence and the punishment – such as a number of days of community involvement in painting pensioners' homes instead of going to prison.

9. **Characterisation**

   Each student chose a character and tried to see the others from their chosen viewpoint, for example:

   Defendant towards magistrate. How would I feel towards the magistrate? Scared? Defiant? Sorry? Would I be feeling guilty about the act or about being in court? What if the magistrate were younger, older or a different gender?

   Cleaner towards public. How would I feel towards people who drop rubbish on my clean floor? Do I sympathise because they're nervous?

Legal aid lawyer: Have I stopped drinking and driving because of the stories I hear in court? Or am I still a heavy drinker? Why? Could this potential conflict in my character be shown in the play somehow?

How about?
- Defendant towards police witness.
- Family in court listening.
- Local newspaper reporter.

10. Improvisation

Each group performed its play with the others acting as the public. One student acted as a reporter and wrote up the case for the school magazine.

11. Career folders

All the information gathered on roles associated with the courts was put into a file: one folder per occupation, available for student browsing. Other queries arose:

What is said when the court is opened?

If you're not a believer in the Bible, what do you use during the swearing in?

Do offenders pay fines immediately?

How big does a court have to be before using a court reporter?

Interested students then set out to discover those answers.

12. Benefits

Students gained a knowledge of court procedures. Attitudes towards the police changed to some feelings of sympathy about the time involved in waiting for traffic cases to come up in court. The court was demystified. Students learnt how to ask specific questions about jobs and get relevant answers. Their questioning techniques improved enormously. They gained experience in gathering information, performing a variety of roles and demonstrating what they had observed without having to write much.

The teachers gained up-to-date information on the legal system which tied in with legal studies, English, drama and careers guidance.

Summary of the Group Approach

1. Choice of setting
2. Background reading
3. Visit to workplace
4. Selection of job role by students
5. 'Mock up' of work-setting within school
6. Performance and discussion of play script
7. Checkout of unresolved questions
8. Brainstorming as students improvised their own workplays
9. Characterisation – the work frustrations and benefits from the chosen character's viewpoint
10. Improvisation in groups
11. Discussion of benefits, and suggested improvements for next time.

Hints for Playmaking

- Setting
- Characters
- Problem or conflict are the ingredients of any good play.

The workplace is an excellent source of drama because there are so many possible conflicts:
- Disagreements over how a job should be tackled
- Accidents with equipment
- Quarrelsome personalities stopping a team effort
- Staff being replaced by AI
- Retrenchment
- Union versus management
- Quality of work versus speed of job.

Some of these conflicts which you may observe will make ideal drama for the plays you will create after visiting the workplace, watching the workers and asking questions.

Checklist for Setting

When you first visit a workplace, concentrate and use all of your senses.
- ☐ First impressions: what do you see, hear, smell, touch and taste?
- ☐ Sketch the layout of the work area. Indicate machinery and fittings such as coffee machines and public seating. Use the correct labels for rooms, such as 'resuscitation', or for equipment, such as 'sterilizer'.
- ☐ Design a rough flow chart of the flow or order in which work is done or the client is looked after.
- ☐ What are the correct names of the various jobs in the organisation? Who is in charge? Are there any on-the-job rules?
- ☐ Observe relationships. Any evidence of teamwork? Any quarrelling or conflict? How are the public treated?
- ☐ When are the busy times? Slack periods? Why?
- ☐ If there is shiftwork, what are the starting and finishing times? Do some shifts overlap?

Getting Inside Your Characters

Here is a checklist which will help you create a character who sounds believable. Work out the details, even if you don't use all of them in the play.

Remember it is dangerous to interview only one person in a particular occupation. You could get a biased account. Talk to at least three different people who all do that same job. Then the character you create in your play script will be a composite of what you've learnt about the workers and your imaginative interpretation.

The character you create is yours.

- ☐ Name
- ☐ Age
- ☐ Birthplace
- ☐ Where did he/she go to school? Feelings about education?
- ☐ Why is this character worth playing?

- ☐ What other types of work has this person tried?
- ☐ Hobbies?
- ☐ See's self as ...
- ☐ Best friend?
- ☐ Present problem. How will this problem get worse? (This provides the conflict from which will come the drama for your play script)
- ☐ Strongest and weakest characteristics
- ☐ Is seen by others as ...
- ☐ Sense of humour?
- ☐ Ambitions?
- ☐ What will the audience like/dislike about this character?

To help you gather facts to create your composite character, here are some useful interview questions.

1. What is the official name of the job you do?
2. Were there any skills you needed before starting this job?
3. What do you like best about the work?
4. Can you suggest some ways in which the job might be improved?
5. Is there any possibility of promotion?
6. Do you think the pay is fair for the work you do? Why?
7. Would you suggest that your child take up this work? Why?
8. Do you have advice for someone considering this job? What would they need to do in preparation for it?
9. Is there much variety in your work?
10. When do you start and when do you finish? Is there any shift work?

Hospital and Medical Areas

Understanding the intricacies of hospital and care careers holds importance in contemporary education. As the healthcare industry continues to evolve, equipping students with insights into these professions not only broadens their career horizons but also instills empathy and compassion.

Learning about hospital and care careers prepares students for the challenges and responsibilities associated with providing healthcare services. It fosters an appreciation for the diverse roles within these sectors, from doctors and nurses to occupational therapists and support staff.

Emergency

> *'On the weekends, the most common casualties are injured sportsmen, scorched barbeque chefs and, as one nurse grimly puts it, people who fillet their feet in the lawnmower.*

Then there are the drug abuse cases (14 cases of legal drug abuse, especially alcohol, for every heroin overdose according to one doctor) and of course, the road smash casualties.

The emergency department can be the busiest place in the hospital ... the treatment area of emergency is all bright lights and whiteness, except for the pale green curtains dividing the sixteen numbered cubicles and the three larger resuscitation areas marked A, B and C.

Patients who are judged not to need immediate treatment in emergency wait to be seen while doctors attend the most urgent cases: the drug overdoses, the serious accident injuries, the patients with heart or respiratory failure ...'

Philip McIntosh, Intern Doctors in the Making

Other Hospital/Medical Work

Nurses and doctors are not the only ones who work in a hospital or in the medical field. Look at these jobs.

Member of hospital gardening and grounds staff

'Patients like to see a bit of colour around the place. So I plant out seedlings, do the weeding and keep them watered.

I have to look after my tools, clean them up and put them away at the end of the day.

I like being outside, in the fresh air.

Have to be a bit of a handyman too.

Still, it's nice if someone says the flowers look good. Sometimes the regulars want to tell you how to grow things. I just smile and keep quiet. Then I do it my way.'

Occupational therapist

'Working with patients in the hospital, I focus on enhancing their daily living skills and promoting independence.

One aspect of my job involves designing personalised rehabilitation activities to improve fine and gross motor skills. I often work with patients on adaptive techniques for tasks like dressing, grooming, and cooking.

It's rewarding to witness their progress and see them regain confidence in their abilities.

I also provide advice to caregivers, to ensure a supportive environment for recovery beyond the hospital setting.'

Interviews

An orderly, working in the Emergency department.

Q. What would you do on a typical day?
A. It depends on which shift. Earlies are from 7 a.m. until 3.30 p.m., afternoons are from 2.30 p.m. until 10.45 p.m., and the late shift, which is the worst, is from 10.45 p.m. until 7 a.m. the next morning. There are two orderlies on each shift.

When we first come in, we sign on. Then we get our count book and count all the trolleys, the intravenous line (IV) poles and the other equipment. Then we stock all the cupboards. By this time, it's about 8 o'clock, so we wait for things to happen.

If anything's missing, we have to go all over the hospital to find it. Sometimes we check for a few days, then realise it's stolen, just like a few wheelchairs from the night shift were once when a couple of drunks were fooling around.

When the patients come in, we push them on the trolleys. If they go to X-ray, we run the X-ray card around.

Anything the nurses or the doctors want, we do. Such as lifting, setting out equipment or changing trolley linen.

Q. What is satisfying about the job?
A. We see a lot of sick people. I like it when they go out feeling better, that's good.

It's a bit frightening when you first start. You don't know where to put yourself. It takes a while to get used to cleaning up the vomit and the blood. It puts you off drinking and driving when you see some of the motor accident victims.

Q. Do patients usually appreciate your help?
A. Usually. Others get a bit upset about waiting. And often they're pretty uptight. You have to learn to be calm.

Q. What skills are needed?
A. Ability to work shifts. Some people can't. Two weeks of earlies, then a week of lates doesn't suit everybody.

You need to be able to take orders from the nurse. Some blokes find that difficult. Even if the nurse is a male nurse.

A Day in the Life of ...

Understanding a workers typical day provides valuable insights into their responsibilities, challenges, and contributions. Here are some of the different roles that you might find around an emergency department.

Paramedic/Ambulance Officer
A standard day might include:
- Ensure all medical equipment and vehicles are ready for emergencies
- Respond promptly to various urgent situations
- Quickly assess patients and gather vital signs at the scene
- Administer first aid, perform procedures and give medications
- Safely transport stabilised patients to emergency and hand over patient for next steps
- Debriefing after a day by discussing cases.

Patient Services Coordinator
A standard day might include:
- Create ordered chaos out of complete turmoil
- Find patients when they're lost somewhere between the waiting room, back corridor, a cubicle, X-ray and home

- Take orders from four doctors, answer three nurses questions and talk on the phone at the same time
- Find staff to do ten sets of observations, six dressings, four ECGs and a dangerous drug injection when they're all busy and the doctor has returned for the third time to ask for the results
- Organise staff breaks
- Find doctors and cubicles when there aren't any
- Explain to hysterical, anxious relatives what is happening and why, and find someone to look after Mrs X's children.

Doctor

A standard day might include:
- Conduct consultations with patients, diagnose medical conditions, and discuss treatment plans
- Visit hospitalised patients, review their progress, and adjust treatment as needed. This is known as medical rounds
- Maintain detailed patient records, ensuring accurate and up-to-date information for effective healthcare management
- Work closely with nurses, specialists and other healthcare professionals
- Stay updated on medical advancement and research
- Handle administrative duties, such as filling out paperwork, responding to emails, and managing appointments
- Engage in community health initiatives and educational programs to promote wellbeing.

Work Flow Chart

During your play, the patients will move around in this order while the other patients are talking. Improvise extra dialogue where necessary. As an example, the emergency triage nurse will always ask the basic list of questions. While in the waiting room, patients may use their mobile phones, have a cup of coffee, talk to other patients or read the notices.

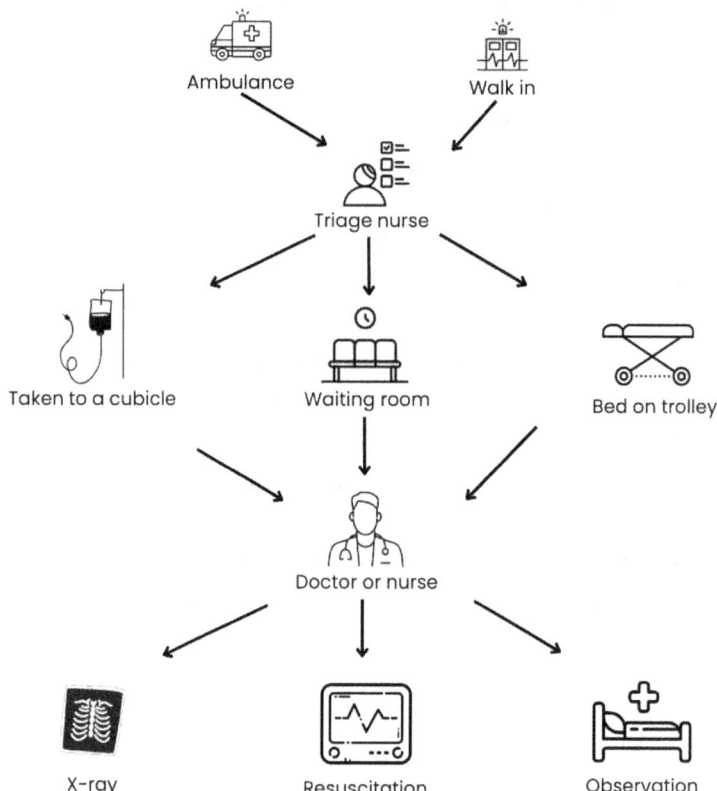

This is the layout of one hospital Accident and Emergency Centre which is usually known as 'Emergency'. You may use this as a guide if you are unable to visit a hospital before starting your play.

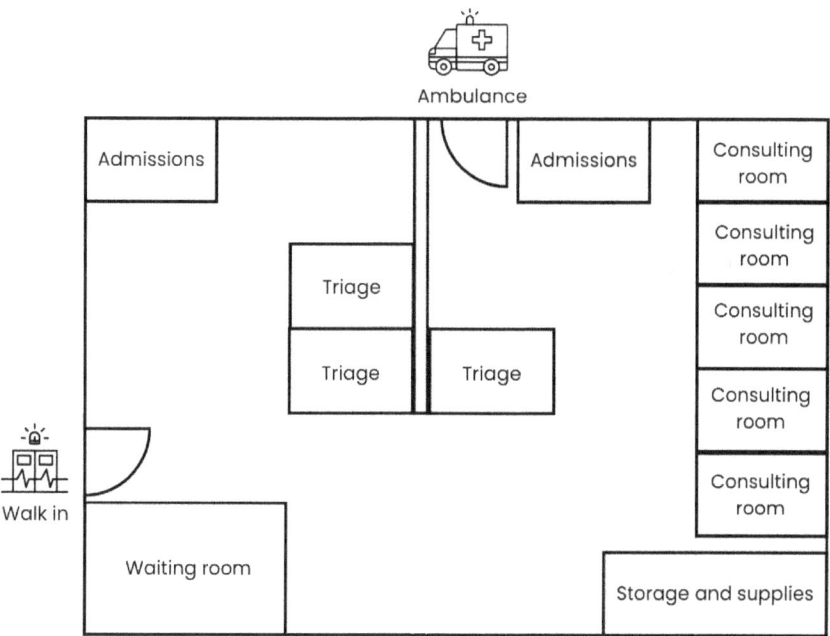

Play: Saturday Night Down in Emergency

Cast
- Hospital orderlies (2) – responsible for moving patients onto trolleys, running messages for the nurses or doctors, cleaning equipment, mopping up and stocking supplies. Need to be strong and quick to obey orders.
- Ward assistant – takes messages for nurse and generally helps around ward. Wears a blue uniform.
- Ambulance officers (2) – give emergency treatment to the sick or injured. After preparation for travel, the ambulance officers transport the patient to hospital. Have to fill in a form on each patient carried.

- Cleaners (2) – 1 male and 1 female (Anna). Do the basic cleaning of floors, toilets, etc, daily. Use a trolley for cleaning equipment.
- Registered general nurse, 3-year trained, white uniform.
- State enrolled nurse, 1-year trained, fawn uniform.
- Student nurse, being trained. Under the supervision of the charge nurse.
- Triage (sorting) nurse – very experienced nurse who writes down patient's complaint and sorts patients into priorities of treatment. Patient cards are colour coded.
- Patient Care Coordinator – in charge of examination cubicles. Talks on loud speaker.
- Resuscitation nurse – in charge of Resuscitation room, where very urgent patients are treated.
- Emergency clerks (2) – at reception, record details of patient to form the hospital record. Check on health fund details.
- Doctors (2) – diagnose and administer medical care. Wear white coats and stethoscopes.
- Hospital switchboard operator.
- Engineer – on call to keep all equipment functioning whether sterilisers, automatic doors, air conditioning or power supplies.
- Police (2)
- Dan Avos – trod on a rusty nail. Impatient: wants to get home to his favourite television program.
- Mr and Mrs Neill – looking for son's lost bag. Very argumentative.
- Anxious woman – ringing from home about injury to cocky.
- Patient in life-threatening situation who arrives in ambulance, which alerts hospital with a Signal 1.
- Yahoos (drunken louts) who escort mate.
- Blue patient who mistakenly dried himself on a new navy towel.
- Mrs Rene Marks arrives by ambulance. Suffering from chest pains. Goes to the Resuscitation room.
- Patients (any number) sitting in waiting room.

Props

- All staff wear identity cards stating name, photo and occupation
- Bag containing old slippers and pyjamas
- Trolleys for moving patients
- Wheelchair
- Seats in waiting room
- Drink machine
- Posters on waiting room wall, e.g. 'Do not leave babies in parked cars. Heatstroke is a potential killer.'
- Triage desk
- Thermometer
- Cards colour-coded for patients:

	Priority	Waiting time	Waiting limit	Types
1	Orange	30 seconds	3 minutes	Severe head injuries Multiple trauma Life-threatening
2	Yellow	5 minutes	30 minutes	Snake bites Unconscious Chest pains
3	Blue/yellow dot	30 minutes	> 60 mins	Needs to be seen by a doctor
4	Blue	60 minutes	> 2 hours	Minor lacerations
5	White	Up to 2 hours	> 4 hours	Could be treated by own doctor later
6	Black	At hospital's discretion	N/A	Needs further assessment

Setting

- Emergency department of a suburban hospital on Saturday before Christmas. Decorations on the windows.
- Husband and wife arguing outside, approach nurse at triage desk, then back away.
- Patient limps through door to triage desk.

Script

DAN AVOS	M'names Dan Avos. Can you help me? I trod on a rusty nail. *(Looks down at foot. Tries to put it on desk.)*
TRIAGE NURSE	When did this happen, Mr Avos?
DAN AVOS	Three weeks ago.
TRIAGE NURSE	Has your doctor seen it?
DAN AVOS	No. I didn't want to bother him on a Saturday night.
TRIAGE NURSE	Three weeks ago exactly? *(Sorts through cards. Takes out white one.)*
DAN AVOS	That's right.
TRIAGE NURSE	*(Patiently)* Could you go across to reception, over there, and our clerk will fill in a few details for your medical record.
DAN AVOS	*(Indignantly)* Aren't you going to fix it straight away?
TRIAGE NURSE	As soon as possible, Mr Avos. There are other people with more urgent need of attention ahead of you. *(Mr Avos looks at waiting room full of patients.)*
DAN AVOS	*(Grumpily)* All right. But I want to get back soon to see my favourite program.
CLERK	We have to fill out a record for each patient. Have you been here before?
DAN AVOS	No. *(Answers all other queries as CLERK asks them)* Name? Address? Mobile phone number? Country of birth?

	Age? Occupation? Religion?
DAN AVOS	What has religion got to do with a nail in m'foot?
CLERK	*(Smiling patiently)* Surname of next of kin? Relationship to you? Their mobile phone number? Benefit fund? Which schedule? *(Does this for each patient who comes in. Patients make up their own responses)*
CLERK	Take a seat, Mr Avos. *(Meanwhile husband and wife approach triage nurse, still arguing.)*
MRS NEILL	Excuse me, nurse. Any news on the bag?
TRIAGE NURSE	Bag?
MR NEILL	We spoke to another nurse last time. Our son was in Emergency Observation last week. Left his bag with his night clothes in it. Now it's gone. Not worth much, but ...
MRS NEILL	*(Interrupting)* At least fifty dollars.
TRIAGE NURSE	All personal belongings are checked either by the patient or two staff members ... But I'll try and find out for you. What was the name?
MR NEILL	Neill.
TRIAGE NURSE	When was he admitted?
MRS NEILL	Last Monday.
TRIAGE NURSE	Perhaps if you take a seat over there. *(Husband and wife still arguing sit in waiting room, talk to other patients about their son.)*

(Emergency phone rings.)

TRIAGE NURSE Emergency. Nurse X speaking.

ANXIOUS MOTHER I was cutting the cocky's wing and it bled.
I went to get the mercurochrome to dab it and my daughter had drunk it. What will I do?

TRIAGE NURSE Bring the child in for treatment.

ANXIOUS MOTHER Yes, but what will I do about the cocky's wing? It won't stop bleeding.

LOUD SPEAKER 'Orderly needed in Room 12 please.'
(Orderly moves quickly. Reappears pushing patient on trolley towards X-ray.)

TRIAGE NURSE Perhaps you could try the vet for the cocky?

ANXIOUS MOTHER Thanks. *(Hangs up)*
(Husband and wife hover again, she pushes him forward. Triage nurse looks up.)

MR NEILL That bag of our son's. It could have been stolen.

TRIAGE NURSE What was in it?

MRS NEILL Those pyjamas alone were worth fifty dollars. Of course I did get them at a sale. Then the slippers, twenty dollars ...

MR NEILL *(Interrupting)* Each slipper.

MRS NEILL And his dressing gown ...

TRIAGE NURSE We're checking for you. Excuse me.
(Signal sounds on radio.)

TRIAGE NURSE Signal 1 from an ambulance. A life-threatening emergency within three minutes of arrival.
(All staff quickly get ready, especially resuscitation room. Ambulance arrives. Ambulance officers come to triage desk. Orderly helps lift patient on to trolley.

	Wheels it into resuscitation room. Lots of drunken noise outside. Yahoos escort mate to triage desk, stand swaying.)
YAHOO	Our mate's a bit crook, nurse. *(Orderly hovers in background, as protection.)*
TRIAGE NURSE	Let me see. Would the rest of you sit down over in the waiting room please? *(Yahoos make nuisances of themselves. Fooling with mobile phone, drink machine and annoying other patients. Lighting cigarettes despite 'No Smoking' notice. Triage nurse looks after Yahoo patient.)*
ORDERLY	There's a No Smoking sign. So please put out your cigarettes.
YAHOO	Why should we? Just give us one good reason!
ORDERLY	Because we're using oxygen and other gases in the resuscitation room and one cigarette might start a fire.
YAHOO	So what? Fire away! Pretty quiet place this. Needs some life.
ORDERLY	Your mate could be in there.
YAHOO	Yeah ... *(Puts out cigarette.)*
ORDERLY	Thank you.
YAHOOS	Hey, nurse. This notice on the drink machine. Says we have to ask a nurse before giving anything to eat or drink to the patient. Reckon we can have a drink, eh?
NURSE	Coffee won't hurt you.
YAHOO	What about something else?

Hospital and Medical Areas 25

LOUD SPEAKER	'Orderly! Room 12 please.'
	(Two nurses unlock door of room with drug cupboard. Lock door behind them. Unlock drug cupboard. Waiting-room patients watch them.)
YAHOO	Don't they trust us? Locking themselves up like that.
PATIENT CARE COORDINATOR	
	The drug cupboard can only be unlocked with two members of staff. It's a precaution.
	(Patient looking rather blue tries to get in the door. Automatic door is stuck. Has to walk around the side.)
ORDERLY	Automatic doors have stuck again. Have to call the engineer.
TRIAGE NURSE	Third time this week. *(Dials number.)*
BLUE PATIENT	*(To orderly.)* Are you the doctor?
ORDERLY	No. I'm the orderly. The Triage nurse is over there. She'll help you first.
PATIENT	Was just having a shower, nurse. Dried myself quickly. Then I noticed.
TRIAGE NURSE	Noticed what?
PATIENT	That I was turning blue.
ORDERLY	*(Watching, smiling.)* Excuse me. Was it a blue towel?
PATIENT	*(Surprised)* Yes ... A birthday present from my girlfriend. Navy blue.
ORDERLY	Better mention that to nurse.
TRIAGE NURSE	*(Smiling)* Blue Dye Syndrome
	(Orderly and nurse smile. Patient begins to understand. Starts laughing. So do others in waiting room.)

ORDERLY	Need a sense of humour around here.
TRIAGE NURSE	Yes.
	(Engineer arrives to fix doors.)
ENGINEER	Pity about that. It was a great program I was watching.
DAN AVOS	Do you watch that too?
ENGINEER	*(Nodding)* Problem about being on call. Always get called out during the interesting bits. Never mind. There you are ... that should work again. Just in time, by the look of things. Here comes another ambulance.
	(Ambulance officers helping elderly woman inside.)
TRIAGE NURSE	What's your name?
MRS MARKS	Mrs Rene Marks
TRIAGE NURSE	Is it spelt R.E.M.A.R.K.S?
MRS MARKS	No. M.A.R.K.S.
TRIAGE NURSE	*(Spelling)* No. M.A.R.K.S.
MRS MARKS	No. My name is Marks. And I want to lie down. My heart feels ... chest pains you know.
	(Triage nurse takes ambulance officers' record while they help patient on to trolley. Orderly also helps lift her.)
AMBULANCE OFFICER	
	Just get comfortable on there, Mrs Marks.
MRS MARKS	Thank you. You've been very helpful.
	(Cleaners pass through, finishing mopping floor. Ward assistant delivers notes to X-ray for Patient Care Coordinator.)
LOUD SPEAKER	'Mr Avos to Cubicle 3 please.'
DAN AVOS	At last.

(Goes to cubicle where he's examined by doctor with nurse in attendance. Resuscitation nurse and other orderly look after Mrs Marks. Husband and wife Neill approach Triage nurse again.)

MR NEILL Excuse me, nurse. Any more news on my son's bag?
With that dressing gown and all, it must have been worth a couple of hundred dollars at least. Is it covered by insurance?

TRIAGE NURSE Anna? *(Calling to female cleaner.)*
Did you see a bag in the observation room last Monday?

ANNA Lots of suitcases ... Get in the way of my cleaning.

MRS NEILL This one was brown and his pyjamas were blue, with pink flowers on them. I know because I bought them at the sale ... er ... at that expensive shop.

TRIAGE NURSE Are you sure, Anna?

ANNA *(Getting upset.)* Is someone saying I steal things? I am honest ... we are all honest here.

TRIAGE NURSE Calm down Anna. We know you. Of course you're honest. Sorry. Mrs Neill, we'll follow it up later.

ANNA Just a minute. Did it have yellow handles?

MR NEILL That's right.

ANNA Then it's still in there. All week, I wondered why so many patients had the same bag. Wait. I'll get it for you.

MRS NEILL Bet she knew all the time.

TRIAGE NURSE Anna is very honest. We trust her completely. You were lucky that she was still on duty.

MRS NEILL	*(Hurriedly)* Of course, the pyjamas were on special … so perhaps they weren't that expensive … *(Anna returns triumphantly with bag.)*
ANNA	Here you are, Madame.
TRIAGE NURSE	Thanks, Anna. *(Accidentally knocks buzzer under desk which rings switch to call police.)*
TRIAGE NURSE	Oh, no! *(Mobile phone rings.)*
SWITCHBOARD	This is the hospital switchboard. I have called the police to come immediately. What is the problem? Or shall I cancel the call? They'll be here within five minutes.
TRIAGE NURSE	Sorry. An accident. Never done that before. Please cancel the emergency call. We don't need help.
MR & MRS NEILL	Thank you nurse. We'll go now.
TRIAGE NURSE	Everything there? Please sign this release form. *(Mr Neill opens case. Raggedy old pyjamas and slippers fall out. Neill stuffs them back quickly.)*
LOUD SPEAKER	'Orderly to cubicle 4.'
TRIAGE NURSE	Very quiet night tonight. Wonder if I'll last until the next shift comes on?

Activities: Suggested Play Scripts

Script 1

Setting
Boiler room of an old hospital

Cast
- Boiler attendant
- Apprentice plumber
- Hospital plumber
- Chief engineer
- Theatre nurse who complains about steriliser not working
- Chef who complains that meals can't be cooked for patients and staff.
- Accountant who complains about the cost of replacing parts

Problem
- Breakdown in boiler room. No steam or hot water. Develop your own play.
- Why has the boiler broken down? Is it anyone's fault or is it worn out?
- Do the workers act as a team, or not 'get along' with each other?
- How will the chief engineer react? Will it be difficult to handle the chef and the theatre nurse?
- Is this the first or the tenth time the boiler has broken down this month?
- What is needed to fix it? Will the cost be high? Will overtime payments be included? Will the staff have to work late?

Script 2

Setting
Geriatric ward of a hospital

Cast
- Orderlies (any number) to help patients move
- Ward attendants
- Domestic staff to clean floors
- State registered nurses
- Doctor
- Ambulance officers
- Patients (any number) who are very frail

Problem
- Fire alarm rings and patients must be evacuated. Some don't want to go. Others think it is just a regular fire drill.

Think about
- What is the correct way to lift a heavy adult without straining the lifter's back?
- What would you do with a panic-stricken person who wouldn't co-operate?
- How would you move bedridden and wheelchaired patients if the lifts and stairs were out of action?

Script 3

Setting

Its the weekend at a large, metropolitan hospital when the work, people and facilities of the institution are on display.

Cast
- All hospital workers plus volunteers
- Patients (any number) and their visitors (any number)

Problem
- The Governor is to make a special visit to the one millionth patient, and present an award to the amazing staff. Just as the Governor arrives the power fails.
- Everyone tries to keep the hospital operating. There is emergency power for the theatre, but not much else.

Supermarket

Gaining insights into supermarket and logistic careers is great for students navigating the contemporary job landscape. These sectors play a pivotal roles in the food supply chain.

Learning about supermarket and logistic careers not only broadens career options, but also develops an awareness of the roles played by various professionals in ensuring seamless product distribution. It equips students with practical knowledge about inventory management, transportation logistics and customer service, offering a holistic view of the interconnected world of supply and demand.

Mocking Up a Supermarket

Most people have shopped in a supermarket. Some may have worked in one on a casual or part-time basis. So it will be fairly easy to mock up the setting.

Have a look at the layout of your local store. Which goods are offered near the check-outs? Are the 'basics' such as meat and milk kept somewhere near the back so customers will have to walk past 'non essentials' and be tempted?

Shoplifting is a problem for many stores and this is one area which could provide drama for your play script.

Some questions to consider:
- How do supermarket workers feel towards shoplifters?
- What is the procedure for stopping a shoplifter?
- How is security organised in a big store?
- Are there any ways of checking that staff are not stealing from the store?
- Why are people attracted to security jobs where they may have to catch shoplifters?

Work Structure in Typical Supermarket

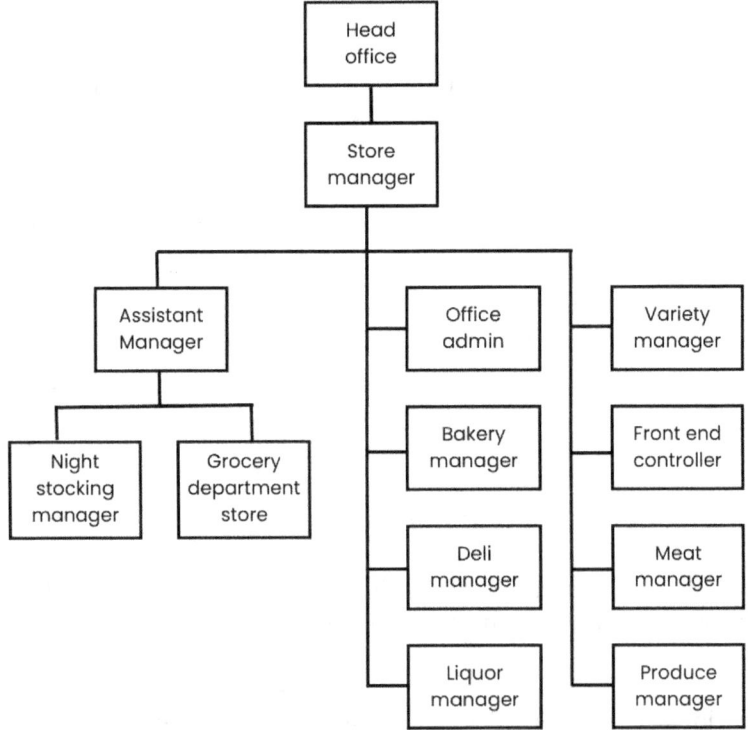

Interviews

Checker – Ruth

'The 11 a.m. to 3 p.m. part-time hours suit me because I have a young family. Only ten minutes for a break about lunchtime, but it's OK if you like dealing with people. Being on your feet all the time is hard and sometimes the public can be rude. One woman said I didn't charge the 'special' price but she'd picked up the wrong brand. That sort of thing can be unpleasant.

Shopping is a hobby for some people. For others, it's just another job. You can tell a lot about the person from the type of food they buy. Such as the junk food types and the healthy ones.

The weight watchers who buy all the low calorie brands and then sneak in bars of chocolate or ice-cream, which they claim is for their kids.

Bargain hunters arrive at 11.55 p.m. on a Saturday, just before discounting dated food. Luckily I'm not here then ...

You have to check cash, so you have to be quick with your fingers and have a good memory for prices.

Promotion is just about non-existent. No job security or superannuation when you're a casual ... but it's close to home.'

Packer – Stan

'I'm the last person a customer speaks to, so I'm very important. They judge the store on whether I was helpful, grumpy or dropped the eggs.

Customer service on exit 9 means I have to help take out the trolley to the car. The customer might have a baby to carry or two trolleys or maybe the packages are awkward for just one person

My job is to stack the frozen food stuff together, so soft things are not underneath. I have to make sure the bags aren't so heavy they break. In the slack times, I round up the trolleys which are left in the car park.'

Activities

1. **Design an Ideal Store**
    Design your ideal store. Questions to ask:
    - Where would you place the most expensive goods?
    - How wide would the aisles be?
    - Are any seats available? Toilets? Wheelchair access?
    - For whom will your store be ideal? Customer? Company?

2. **Storefront Observer Challenge**
    In this activity, students will embark on a 'Storefront Observer Challenge' to keenly observe and analyse the dynamics within a retail store. Each student will select a store of their choice and spend a designated period silently observing customer interactions, staff engagement, and overall store operations. They will take notes on visual merchandising, customer service, and any unique aspects that catch their attention. After the observation period, students will present their findings to the class, discussing the store's layout, marketing strategies, and the overall customer experience.

Job descriptions

Understanding a worker's typical day provides valuable insights into their responsibilities, challenges, and contributions. Here are some of the different roles that you might find around a supermarket.

Store Cleaning Assistant

Monday and Tuesday
1. Fill sugar carriers (shop and storeroom)
2. Clean lunchroom
3. Clear and clean tables
4. Clean and fill coffee machine
5. Sweep and mop floor
6. Clean any chrome
7. Sweep stairs to lunchroom

Wednesday and Thursday
1. Process stock
2. Empty bales
3. Clean and tidy cleaning depot
4. Dust night crew tables
5. Empty check-out bins
6. Sweep out
7. Generally tidy up
8. Remove and process stock from check-outs
9. Clean up cigarette areas
10. Empty green bags
11. Find and return trolleys

Variety Department Daily Checklist

Morning routine
a. Dusting (stock and shelves)
b. Shelf cleaning
c. Straightening stock
d. J hooks full

Merchandising
a. End displays (ticketing and stock)
b. Tables (ticketing and stock)
c. Sales opportunities (talking tickets, tie ins etc.)

Paperwork
a. Bulletins processed
b. Invoices (priced, checked and processed daily)

The Variety Department is where all goods other than food are stored. It would include items from bottle openers to bed-linen.

Produce Department Checklist

	Item	Checked ☑	Comments
1	Window banners	☐	
2	Displays full	☐	
3	Racking standards	☐	
4	Housekeeping	☐	
5	Rotation of stock	☐	
6	Plastic bags available	☐	
7	Items sprayed	☐	
8	Stock condition	☐	
9	Temperature of cases	☐	
10	Price check	☐	
11	Lighting	☐	
12	Tissues	☐	
13	Pricelists	☐	
14	Scales	☐	
15	Distress action	☐	
16	Clean tickets/prices	☐	
17	Ice	☐	
18	Baskets	☐	
19	Red spots	☐	
20	Profit lines	☐	
21	Free fruit for children visitors	☐	
22	Merchandising for extra sales	☐	
23	Recipes	☐	
24	Equipment	☐	
25	Variety tie-ins	☐	

Butcher

For sales
- Provide cutting list for meat rooms
- Customer relations
- Display upkeep-recipes, talking tickets, flags, stick-on labels
- All items available on display
- Correct display methods
- Stock rotation (display cases and stockroom)
- All advertised items on display
- Control of presentation standards-danger areas:
  a. Poorly packed meat
  b. Badly cut meat
  c. Excessively fat cuts
  d. Dark meats
  e. Poorly wrapped items
  f. Shop-soiled packs
  g. Blood-stained labels
  h. Incorrect pricing
  i. Incorrect scaling
  j. Poor quality

Night display preparation
- Housekeeping
- Wrapping machine area
- Display case upkeep (back ledge and front panels)
- Maintain trading floor area

Expense control
- Checking case temperatures
- Care of case and maintenance of equipment
- Expense item control

General
- Abide by weights and measures requirements
- Liaison with department manager on trends
- Satisfactory customer service
- Compliance with all health regulations

Dairy Manager (and Deep Freeze Manager)

Sales and profits
- Complete stock movements records
- Ordering and maintaining stock of all items available
- Damaged goods processing
- Pull date and ID code
- Checking against invoices all merchandise received
- Accurate and punctual paperwork
- Stock rotation (display and reserve)
- Receiving and storing of merchandise
- All advertised items on display
- Control over slow moving items
- Correct distress selling
- Maintenance of fresh merchandise
- Merchandising for sales and profits
- Pricing accuracy (retail and position)
- Price changes
- Product knowledge
- Planned production

Expense control
- Checking case temperatures
- Keep doors to refrigerated rooms closed
- Care and maintenance of equipment

Housekeeping
- Cool room cleaning of walls, floor, doors and fans
- Maintain floor areas
- Maintain work areas
- Display case (coils and fans)

General policy
- Compliance with all health regulations
- Staff appearance as per requirements
- Satisfactory customer service
- No baskets or trolleys left in refrigerated rooms

Office Administrator

Areas of responsibility include:
- Complete security over all monies, confidential information, records and company equipment
- Loyalty and responsibility to the store manager and the company
- Daily balancing of cash register and safe monies
- Preparation of paperwork necessary for accounting procedures
- Maintaining price books
- Issuing staff salary notifications (only if payroll was completed by another employee)
- Maintaining staff files
- Preparing money for banking
- Following correct banking procedures
- Take phone calls to the store
- Answer customer complaints where necessary
- Keep records up-to-date
- Record all store use items
- Control miscellaneous cash flow (petty cash, kiddie rides)
- Keep safe, office drawers and working area in a clean and tidy condition
- Train a second person for 'back-up' purposes
- Do register cash pick-ups and change runs
- Answer price checks
- Maintain high morale and enthusiasm among employees

Night Stocking Manager

Sales
- Accurate price marking
- Correct stacking (skyline, to price beading, flatten out)
- Correct tray cutting
- Repairing loose labels
- Rotation of stock (price changes and general stock)
- Check warehouse load accurately
- Process broken or damaged stock

- Maintaining product facings
- Price all reserve stocks
- Code all reserve stock cartons

Expense control
- Training and development of people (counselling and evaluation)
- Care and maintenance of equipment
- Restroom and toilet lights off when possible
- Staff productivity and discipline
- Proper control over store lighting
- Store expense items
- Correct production methods
- Forward planning

Housekeeping
- Leave shop floor ready for trading
- Leave stockroom ready for incoming loads
- Fixtures cleaned before filling
- Maintaining marking and cutting table
- Return equipment to designated place after use
- Health regulation requirements
- Janitorial control

General policy
- Compliance with health regulations
- Neat and clean staff appearance
- Security of equipment, property and stock during shift
- Holding meeting with department employees monthly
- Fill out nightly and weekly reports
- Secure night crew purchases as policy dictates
- Uphold company name and standard when in charge of store
- Routine bag checks of staff
- An awareness of applicable company policies and union requirements
- Encourage high morale and enthusiasm
- Inventory control awareness

Suggested Play Scripts

Using the information provided in the job profiles and what you have learnt from watching at your local store and interviewing supermarket employees, try creating your own plays.

The three play scripts are only suggestions. You may find some interesting stories during the interviews which you would prefer to blend into your own play.

Script 1

Setting

Opening day in a new store. Banners and balloons everywhere.

Cast

- Demonstrators of food – giving away free samples
- Clown wandering around with balloons
- Checkout cashiers
- Packers
- Customers – (any number) determined to collect bargains
- Reporter – from local paper looking for a story angle
- Photographer – trying to take some casual shots, but everyone keeps posing for the camera
- Manager of store, worried that not all goods have arrived on time
- Store assistants – any number in various departments)
- Catwoman – carrying several of her cats
- Cleaner – who hates cats.

Problem

Fresh fish has been advertised as a special at 10 dollars a kilo, but the fish hasn't arrived. Customers are cross and staff begin to offer tinned fish instead. Someone discovers fishing lines in one of the aisles. Old catwoman brings her cats for the cheap fish, but animals are not permitted in the store. What will happen about the fishing lines? Who will use them? How?

Script 2

Setting

Just before closing time. A suburban supermarket.

Cast

- Bargain hunting customers (any number)
- Butchers who are marking down the price of meat which cannot be refrozen
- Delicatessen assistants
- Part-time packers who are quickly filling the shelves which are almost empty. Some work on the checkouts, packing for customers
- Trolley person who collect discarded trolleys from outside and returns them to the store
- Store security who is checking on shoplifting
- Shoplifters (any number)
- Fruit and vegetable assistants marking down fruit which will not keep over the weekend.

Problem

Shoplifter hides items inside bag. Store security suspects and follows. Items start to fall out.

Power failure. Lights go out. Electric checkouts won't work. Freezers stop. Automatic doors won't open.

How will they cope?

Script 3

Setting

Night stocking at a supermarket in a big country town.

Cast

- Night stocking manager – see job descriptions for more information
- Night crew of packers (any number)
- Cleaners (any number)
- Night crew trainer who is rather bossy
- New employee who doesn't like being told what to do. Has worked in another store and thinks he knows everything. Likes to play practical jokes.

Problem

New employee plays a joke on staff. But things go wrong and the joke leads to someone being shut in the freezer.

Fantasy: Talking to Trolleys

Shopping trolleys are important and expensive pieces of equipment in a store. But sometimes they appear to have minds of their own. Imagine entering a science fiction type of world where the trolleys are in control.

This is what the writer of 'Talking to Trolleys' suspects.

Gardeners talk to plants. Dr Doolittle conversed with animals. I can talk to supermarket trolleys.

'Squeak Bang' means 'Get out of my way or I'll ram you.'

'Swark Thud' means 'We're heading for the peanut butter too.'

Certain skills are necessary to survive in supermarket land. A thick wallet helps. So does not packing the ripe watermelon under the 10 kg potato bag. But the greatest skill is being able to communicate with trolleys in their own language.

'Erk Squawk' means 'I have a bias to the left.'

It is polite to know that.

Until recently I actually thought that customers controlled their shopping routes. Then I overheard a trolleyspeak conversation.

Just near the frozen peas section, another trolley crashed into mine.

'Sorry,' I said automatically.

'Sorry,' said the other woman helplessly.

Then my trolley squeaked all by itself. The other trolley replied. They were talking angrily.

I wasn't crazy because the other woman noticed too.

'Are they talking to each other?'

'I think so.'

There was a pattern to the noises.

Since then, I have looked and listened. You may think that trolleys all look the same, jammed together at the entrance. But they are not.

The Chief Ankle Rammer is usually the trolley littered with orange peel, empty cigarette cartons and used tissues. This deliberate camouflage reduces his daily trips to a minimum. However, if he is chosen, he bad-temperedly rams any customer with bare legs. Running over thongs is his speciality.

Eccentric trolleys refuse to cover certain aisles. The vegetarian trolley won't go near the meat counter, despite the strongest push from his customer.

The diet trolley has a permanent route between the Weight Watchers' lemonade and the lettuce display. She gives passing trolleys an up-to-the minute kilojoule count.

At first, I wondered if there were a hierarchy. Did a full trolley rank over an empty one? Was it better to be loaded with prawns and avocados or Vegemite and apples? Were child passengers a liability?

Last Wednesday, I spoke my first few phrases in trolleyspeak.

'Swauk Eh?' meaning 'Would you like to come shopping with me?'

'Swauk Eh?' came the reply from the first trolley parked at the entrance.

'Do you have a left or right bias?'

'Middle of the road.' came the reply.

We set off. My squeaking guide treated me like a naive tourist in a world where wheels dominate.

'Watch out for him. He lets soup cubes through his wires'

The customer pushing looked quite pleasant. Should I warn him about his cubes? Too late. We were in amongst the soap powders now. Instead of concentrating on specials, nutrition or my shopping list, my ears were alert for trolleyspeak.

'Got a bad trolley?' the woman customer smiled sympathetically at me. 'Making a lot of noise.'

I didn't dare agree.

'Squarl Squealll.'

Then I realised about trolley power. Secretly, they have been controlling the eating patterns of this nation.

In the future, unless humans learn trolleyspeak, we won't survive in the new world war.

Our local supermarket has a large, sloping carpark. One hot, windy day, there were very few cars parked. Abandoned trolleys dominated. Hot air blew up into a wind which pushed the trolleys to the left and then to the right.

At the time I didn't realise I was watching a union meeting.

It looked like an accident when three trolleys rolled in unison to crash into a parked car.

Now, I'm not so sure!

Use the ideas in 'Talking to Trolleys' as the basis of your own fantasy sci-fi drama.

Setting

Store where the trolleys are in control. Their language is 'Trolleyspeak' They make the customers do what they wish.

Cast

- Customers who are confused by what is happening
- Staff who are worried
- Customer who already speaks five languages, tries to learn 'trolley speak' and act as an interpreter.

Problem

The trolleys are annoyed by something the customers have done.

Dramatic Problems to be Solved

- How can you script your play? Will actors play trolleys?
- Would it work better as a radio play?
- What about using a 'voice over' technique, with one student playing the narrator?
- Will you have names for individual trolleys?
- Will the play be a political satire?
- How will you choreograph the movement of the trolleys? Which way will they go? Will the customers try to push them?
- Why might the trolleys be protesting? Tired of being abused? Tired of being left out in the rain? Annoyed at being adapted into billycarts, hanging plant holders or dumped on the rubbish tip?
- The play will need a climax. Can you think of a 'twist' on which to end your play? Will trolleys be replaced by video display terminals and home deliveries when customers shop by screen?

Writing a Group Story: Trolleypower

Outline

Part-time jobs are hard to get. When Chris starts collecting trolleys at Kmart, he is very happy for two weeks. Then some kids from his school start shoplifting.

Chris wants to tell Judy, the boss, but the kids stop him. If he tells, they will 'get' Chris and his sister Gaby.

Chapter 1

'Look out!'

The runaway trolley took off. It ran down the hill, just missed the V. W. and hit the fat lady.

She dropped her supermarket bags.

Splat!

That was the eggs!

Then her green apples rolled away.

I watched from the trolley bay. Should I help? Shoppers are strange. They blame staff for everything. Even if it was the wind pushing the trolley. I know. I've been collecting trolleys part-time at Kmart for two weeks now.

Shoppers don't realise that trolleys have minds of their own.

That trolley came from over here. She's sure to think it was mine.

Oh well. Trolleys are my job.

'Need a hand?' I offered. Four of the apples looked to have turned brown. I picked them up.

'No ... no ... I can do it' she puffed as she grabbed the apples from me. The 'I am a weight watcher' T-shirt she was wearing was a tight fit.

Quickly, she stuffed the apples into the bag. She didn't want me to see what was inside. Was she hiding something?

Was she a shop lifter?

'I'll carry that to the car for you' I said.

Celery stuck out of the broken bag.

Before she could say no, I took it. The bag felt cold.

She pointed to the green car. I waited while she opened the boot. Just as I put the bag in, it broke. Under the celery were the hidden things. There were cream buns, an ice cream cake, six Mars bars and a bag of chips

But the docket was there too.

She looked at me and her face went red. She tugged at her T-shirt. She knew that I knew.

She wasn't a shop-lifter, just someone cheating on her diet.

'Thanks' she said quickly and shut the boot.

'That's all right.' I walked back to the trolley bay. The wind was still strong enough to blow away more trolleys.

Later, I met some real shoplifters.

This is the end of Chapter 1. Using the outline given earlier, try writing the next chapter as a group activity.

Perhaps you could act out Chapter 2, discuss improvements and then rewrite it. Each member of the group could be responsible for producing another act or chapter.

Some questions to consider:
- Who might the shoplifters be?
- What conflict does Chris face? Should he inform on school mates?
- How does Chris feel about his sister Gaby?
- Is finding part time work difficult?
- Can you think of a better title than 'Trolley Power'?

Now it will become your dramatised story.

Perhaps the final version could be printed, published and put into your school library.

Court

Exploring careers in the legal and justice professions, particularly within the context of a court, is valuable. It provides students with a understanding of the legal system, fostering a sense of civic responsibility and respect for the rule of law.

Learning about court and legal careers not only introduces students to roles like lawyers, judges and legal clerks but also sheds light on the workings of the justice system. This knowledge helps cultivate critical thinking, ethical reasoning and an appreciation for the principles that underpin our society. Additionally, exposure to legal and justice careers opens doors to potential paths for those considering roles in advocacy, law enforcement or public service.

Procedure for a Day in Court

- See the Clerk of Courts (Bench Clerk) who will tell you where to sit
- Wait until your name is called for your case. If you must leave the court to go to the toilet or for any other reason, tell one of the court

staff or the police officer on duty at the door. Missing your case is serious
- Once the court starts, listen for your name, move to the front of the court. The clerk will show you where to stand. Call the Magistrate either 'sir' or 'your worship'
- The charge or charges will be read out by the Clerk. If there is anything you do not understand, ask the magistrate
- The Magistrate or Clerk will ask if you plead 'guilty' or 'not guilty.' You might decide to plead guilty but tell the Magistrate that you do not agree with part of the charge. For example, you might admit stealing some of the articles, but not all of them
- The prosecution has to try to prove beyond reasonable doubt that you are guilty of the offence
- A plea of not guilty means you deny the truth of the charge read out in court, or that you believe there is not enough evidence that you committed the offence
- A plea of guilty means you admit the truth of the charge read out in court
- A police prosecutor will call for the evidence against you from the police involved and any other witnesses
- You or your lawyer may question what any witness has said.

Day's List Outside the Magistrates' Court

Informant	Defendent	Charge	Barrister	Court
Clarke	Kilsby	Unlicensed driver	Jones	1
Menos	Davis	Unlicensed driver	Cohen	3
Smith	Boyko	Exceeding 0.05	Edwards	2
Morris	Weightman	Breach of probation	Amarilli	4

A Flow Chart of Proceedings

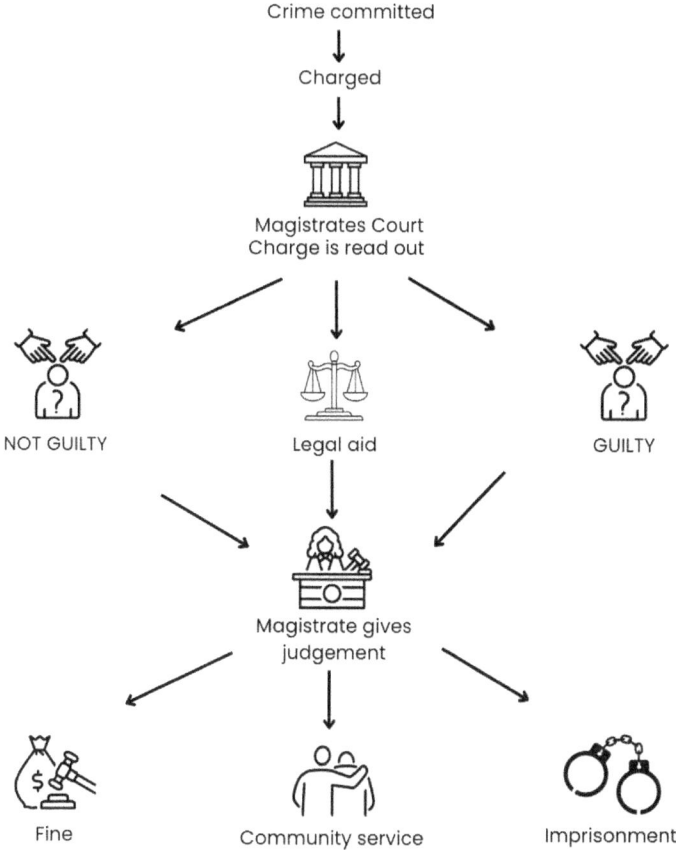

Interviews

Legal Aid

Legal aid plays a role in ensuring access to justice for individuals who may face financial constraints in navigating the legal system. In a court setting, legal aid provides support by offering legal representation, advice and assistance to those who cannot afford private legal services. This assistance helps level the playing field, ensuring that individuals have a fair opportunity to present their case, understand legal processes and exercise their rights. Legal aid organisations often focus on issues related to social justice, human rights and equality. By facilitating access to legal resources, legal aid contributes significantly to upholding the principles of justice and ensuring that individuals receive a fair and impartial hearing in court.

Court Welfare Officer

'Before the court begins each day, I go to the city watchhouse and give a newspaper, toilet articles and clean clothing, from the Salvation Army to those who need them. I send messages to families, arrange accommodation and fares home for people on bail and organise legal aid. Alternatively, if that is refused, I'll speak on the person's behalf to the magistrate.

Part of my job is to explain the accused's circumstances and background to the magistrate to help him determine the appropriate penalty. If the offender is sent to trial, I'll speak on his behalf at the County or Supreme Courts.

Sometimes prisoners who are 'under the weather' abuse me. And it's disappointing to see the same faces so often. The youth of the offenders is frightening too. Sixty per cent of people who are charged before the court are under 25 years old.'

Brigadier Wally Bryant, Salvation Army
Officer and Court Welfare Officer

Police Constable

Imagine you are a new member of the police force on your first court appearance for the prosecution.
- How will you prepare yourself?
- Do you know what to say?
- Who might help you?
- How do you feel towards the magistrate? The accused? The witnesses?

Here's one constable's point of view:

> *'Yes, there is a lot of variety in my job, but I also spend too much time in court. The first time I was really nervous – a bit worried that I'd get all the formal phrases wrong. But you can ask to refer to your notes. Sometimes you have to. It was so long since the offence and there may have been dozens in between.*
>
> *No, I don't feel antagonistic towards the accused. It depends what they have done. I try to stay calm most of the time, I guess. Most people are a bit overcome by the atmosphere of the court, especially if it's their first time.*
>
> *'The ones who plead guilty are the more straightforward cases, but it's still hard when it's your day off. You don't have to wear uniform then, but it eats into your day, especially when your case is down the list.*
>
> *There are lots of traffic and drink driving offences. Some just agree it's a fair thing. They just got caught. When they've hurt or killed someone else that's a different matter.'*

Bail

If the accused has been in custody (been in jail overnight or longer) bail may be sought. Bail is money put up as a guarantee that the person will appear in court on the agreed date and time. The magistrate sets bail according to the seriousness of the crime and the resources of the accused. Sometimes, applications for bail are refused.

If the accused is already in custody on a prior charge, he will be escorted by a policeman or warden. Don't forget to include the extra cast member.

Play: I Went to Court This Morning

Cast
- Magistrate – hears arguments and evidence. Decides on a suitable sentence and announces the fine, reprimand or imprisonment
- Bench clerk – needs to be very efficient. Usually wears a suit. Opens the court, swears in witnesses, keeps lists of people appearing and helps the magistrate with the paperwork
- Court usher – keeps order in the waiting room and other courts. Announces cases and calls witnesses. Checks that court lists are posted on the notice board. Arranges furniture in the court and delivers files to the correct courts
- Marshall (Sheriff) – serves summonses. Escorts prisoners to and from court or from one prison to another
- Prosecutor – police person who presents the case for the prosecution. Not always a lawyer but has legal training
- Barrister – a lawyer who appears in court on behalf of the client.
- Legal aid lawyer – an independent barrister provided by legal aid for people unable to afford their own lawyer.
- Defendant/accused – person accused of a crime.
- Court welfare officer – often a Salvation Army officer. Speaks on behalf of the accused. Talks about the person's family background and circumstances
- Police witness for the prosecution. Usually in uniform and often from the traffic branch
- Clerk-cashier – receives the fines and issues a receipt
- Reporter – looking for stories for the local newspaper
- Cleaner – keeps court rooms clean. Uses a trolley packed with mops and dusters
- Public – friends, witnesses and interested people who sit on the public seats in court, listening

Props
- Chairs, files, dock.

Setting

- For the first run through, actors may prefer to wear job labels or T-shirts printed with their occupation

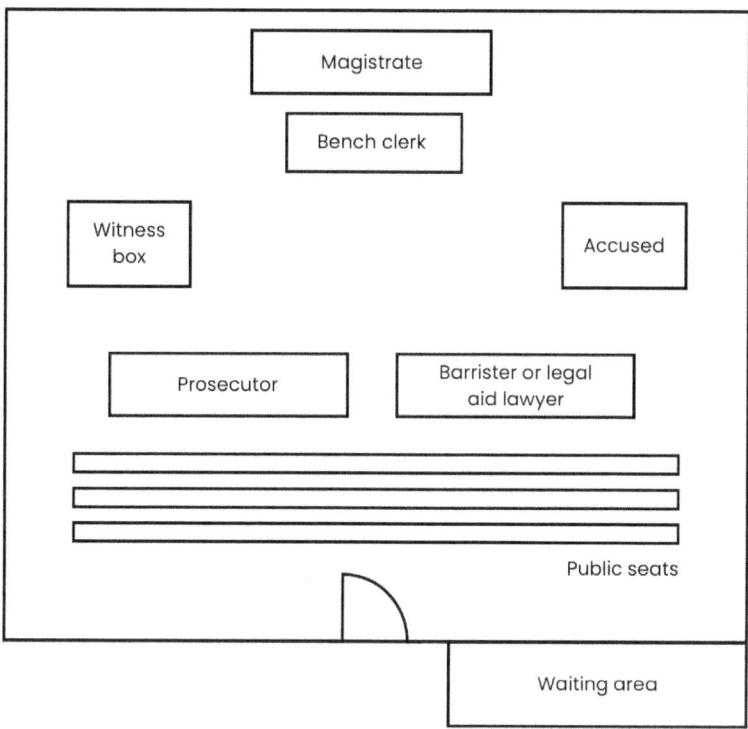

Script

Cleaner is just finishing the floor. Usher pins list of cases on notice board. Moves chairs into court 1. Public gather around list.

CLEANER	What's the rush?
USHER	Big list today. Got to make sure there are enough chairs.
FREDERICKS	Excuse me. Where do I go?
USHER	I don't know, Madam. What's your name?
FREDERICKS	Fredericks. Mrs Jane Fredericks. *(Usher checks list.)*

USHER	There's no Fredericks on today.
FREDERICKS	Oh. There shouldn't be, either. It's my brother-in-law. Alan. Had too much to drink on Saturday, at the wedding and .... *(Usher checks list again.)*
USHER	No Alan here.
FREDERICKS	Oh no. Alan is his first name.
USHER	*(Patiently)* What's his surname?
FREDERICKS	Pappas.
USHER	Alan Pappas. Court 1. Over there.
FREDERICKS	Thank you. *(Bench clerk races into court 1 with lots of files. Drops a few. Policeman on door duty helps pick them up. Clerk gets magistrate's and his own desk in order. Public wander into seats. Police and barristers arrive. Alan Pappas meets his sister-in-law, unwillingly. Some of the accused and witnesses arrive. All look at clock. Magistrate enters.)*
BENCH CLERK	Silence. All stand please. *(Magistrate bows to legal practitioners. They bow back.)*
BENCH CLERK	The Smithstown Magistrates' Court is now open. *(Everyone sits down.)*
BENCH CLERK	Alan Pappas.
USHER	*(Calls out in waiting room.)* Alan Pappas. Pappas enters the accused's box.
BENCH CLERK	Is your name Alan Pappas?
PAPPAS	*(Nodding)* Yes.
BENCH CLERK	You are charged with exceeding .05 blood alcohol limit, on December 13th.

MAGISTRATE	Do you understand the charge?
PAPPAS	Yes, your worship.
MAGISTRATE	How do you plead?
PAPPAS	Guilty, your worship.
MAGISTRATE	I record the plea of guilty. Could we have the facts now, please?
POLICE PROSECUTOR	I should like to call on a witness, Police Constable Brian Nason. *(Constable Nason steps into the witness box and takes up the Bible in his right hand.)*
BENCH CLERK	Take the Bible in your right hand and repeat, I swear by almighty God that the evidence I shall give in this case shall be the truth, the whole truth and nothing but the truth. *(Constable repeats this.)*
CONSTABLE	My name is Brian Neil Nason. I'm a police constable attached to Smithtown Police station. May I refer to my notes your worship?
MAGISTRATE	Yes.
CONSTABLE	On Saturday 13th December, I was proceeding in a northerly direction on Main Street, Smithtown when I saw a motor vehicle LWR 345 travelling at an excessive speed across the double lines. When I stopped the driver, he said his name was Alan Pappas and agreed to accompany me to the police station. At the station he was tested and found to have a blood alcohol level of 1.0.
MAGISTRATE	Thank you constable. You may sit down. Is there anything to be said on the accused's behalf?

ACCUSED'S BARRISTER My client had just been married earlier that afternoon your worship. And a wedding is normally a time of celebration.

MAGISTRATE Usually.

ACCUSED'S BARRISTER My client is a self-employed builder, your worship. To lose his licence would mean his work would be severely affected. He would have to employ a chauffeur, as his new bride doesn't drive. And he has three men working for him. They would lose their jobs.

MAGISTRATE Drinking and driving do not mix. And the reading was a high one.

BARRISTER Yes, your worship. But my client was most cooperative with the police.
(Magistrate fiddles with papers on desk. Writes something.)

MAGISTRATE Was he cooperative constable?
(Constable returns to the witness stand.)

CONSTABLE Yes, your worship. Even when the confetti fell out of his pockets on the police station floor. He offered to sweep it up if someone would find him a broom.

MAGISTRATE *(Smiling)* And where was the bride during this time?

CONSTABLE Gone home to get changed, your worship. Apparently, she had a bottle of champagne spilt over her going away outfit. She went home to get another dress.

MAGISTRATE Why weren't they travelling together? Surely not quarrelling already?

BARRISTER	No your worship. They had arranged to meet at her house.
MAGISTRATE	I see. *(Writes on papers. Stamps them. Looks up.)* Despite the fact that it was your wedding day, to drink and drive is foolish. Surely your best man could have driven you.
BARRISTER	My client's son was his best man. Not 18 yet.
MAGISTRATE	I see. Any previous convictions?
PROSECUTOR	None, Sir.
MAGISTRATE	I see. Since you are unlikely to marry again …
PAPPAS	My fourth marriage sir.
MAGISTRATE	Then this circumstance is not likely to occur again, I hope. Pay $200 to a charity. A stay of 7 days for payment. And a good behaviour bond for twelve months. You may sit down. *(Bench clerk scurries around, presents Pappas with a form to sign.)*
BENCH CLERK	Noel Jones.
USHER	Noel Jones! *(Noel Jones enters the accused's box.)*
BENCH CLERK	Noel Jones is charged with the theft of five crystal goblets from Woolworths stores on 5th November, 2023.
MAGISTRATE	Do you understand the charge?
NOEL JONES	Yeah.
MAGISTRATE	How do you plead?
NOEL JONES	Didn't do it. Not guilty.

Finish this play and try to include as many of the cast as possible.

Activities

Script 1

Setting
Magistrates' Court

Cast
- Magistrate
- Clerk of Courts
- Police prosecutor
- Accused
- Accused's barrister
- Witness for the prosecution
- Public (at least three people, two related to the accused)
- Policeman on door duty

Charge
- Exceeding .05 %
- Driving dangerously

Plea
Guilty

a. This is the first case of the day. Court starts at 10 o'clock. Act out the court scene.
    - Is the accused male or female? How old? Any other convictions? Why did the crime occur?
    - What are the magistrate's feelings about this particular type of crime?
    - In summing up, what will be stressed?
    - What is an appropriate sentence?

    Allow the public to make their comments on the conduct of the case.

b. Using the same charge, change roles and act it out again.
    Notice how some people will interpret the same events differently.

Case 1

Nineteen-year-old girl charged with shoplifting in a city store. Goods to the value of $550. Caught trying to walk out wearing four sets of clothes. She's been unemployed for 18 months and her family isn't interested in her.

Case 2

Twenty-six-year old man charged with assault by kicking at a football match. He attacked an opposing team's supporter just after the final siren. Also charged with indecent language.

Case 3

Unlicensed driver with an unregistered vehicle stopped by police outside hospital emergency where he had taken a friend with a cut leg. Claimed it was a good samaritan act.

Case 4

Two men, 45 and 48, both charged with arson because on January 22nd they intentionally and without lawful excuse destroyed ten houses by setting fire to them.

Each was also charged with offences under the Country Fire Authorities Act of using a petrol-driven grinding tool in the open air without having erected a guard of fire resistant material to prevent a fire being caused by ignition of sparks; that they used a petrol-driven grinding tool in the open without having cleared or kept wet the immediate area in a radius of 150 centimetres sufficiently to prevent the spread of fire; that they used a petrol-driven grinding tool in the open air without having available a reticulated water supply or an effective water spray pump with a capacity of not less than nine litres.

1. Choose one of the cases listed
2. Work out who will be involved if the plea is guilty:
   - Magistrate?
   - Accused?
   - Bench clerk?
   - Police prosecutor?

- Accused's barrister or legal aid officer?
- Court welfare officer?

If the plea is not guilty, witnesses will be involved.
- Prosecution witnesses? Defence witnesses?
- Court reporter for a local human interest story?

3. Decide who will say what. A certain legal sequence must be followed and here the flow chart should be useful.
4. What about some dramatic interruptions?
   Fire drill/alarm? Member of the public faints? Accused tries to run away? Adjournment for lunch and someone doesn't come back? What could be happening in the waiting room? Could the lights fail? Maybe it's April fools' day and someone is playing a joke?
5. Work out your own play.

Emergency Services

A career in the emergency services opens the door to a dynamic and rewarding professional journey. This field offers the opportunity to be at the forefront of aiding and protecting communities during their most challenging times. Whether as a paramedic, firefighter or police, individuals in these roles benefit from a sense of purpose that comes with making a direct, positive impact on people's lives.

Play: Fire on Trial

A partly scripted improvisation, using simple masks, which may be performed in the classroom before a student audience or recorded by a student television crew.

Cast
- Judge – who must pronounce an appropriate sentence after the jury has given its verdict.
- Fire – who is being accused. Wears a fire mask. Fire can be acted by a small chorus.

- Witnesses – who speak for or against fire
  - Witness I, house fire victim who died in fire, and who tells how and why fire destroyed his or her home and body
  - Witness 2, fire user, someone who has used fire well and tells of its good uses. Possible characters might be: Sunny Day, the heating engineer; Pierre Le Gourmet, a chef; Mr Water Gum, the gum tree; Chief Fire Officer Battle or the Head of the Boora Boora which uses fire well
  - Witness 3, a fire officer who has fought many big fires and who tells of the dangers when fire is not understood and of the mistakes made by people, not by fire
  - Witness 4, child fire-bug, Smoky Sparks, who lit a fire and was terrified by the speed at which it grew. Hair and eyelashes were burnt off
- Four fire extinguishers – red, blue, red with black, and red with white, explain their colour codes and contents for different types of fires
- Smoke – could tell, in a sequel to this play, why they are a greater danger to people than Fire
- Jury – any number; or these parts could be played by the audience. The Jury must decide if Fire is guilty of destroying lives, homes and businesses,

Props
- Actors may like to wear plain black clothes and use masks to suggest the character. Masks may be simple or elaborate, for example:
  - Judge could wear a wig attached to the mask
  - Fire officer could wear a helmet
  - Child might wear a stocking over their head, to suggest no hair
  - Fire extinguishers could display their colour codes. They might wear large cardboard boxes.

Simulating Fire and Smoke
One of the challenges is to simulate fire and smoke on stage or in the classroom without the danger of real flames.

Listed below are some ideas that have been used in other student productions:
- Actors in red tights with red and yellow fringes attached along the sleeves
- Red and yellow cellophane streamers
- Actors moving like flames growing
- Smoke shown by blue, grey or white cotton wool or streamers
- A red balloon with streamers attached, puffed by a fan
- Red T-shirts with 'FIRE' labels.

Setting
- A courtroom. Improvise using classroom furniture.

Script

JUDGE	Welcome to my court. Today Fire is on trial. Fire is accused of burning and destroying many people and places. Witnesses will speak about what Fire has done to them. Some will speak of the good things. Others will speak of the bad things which Fire has done.
FIRE	*(Interrupting)* Will I have a chance to defend myself?
JUDGE	Yes. You will be given a chance to reply after each witness speaks. Then I will give my verdict. You may be sentenced to imprisonment or you may be set free in the community. Bring in the first witness. *(HOUSE FIRE VICTIM stands.)*
VICTIM	My name is ... I live at ... Sorry, I used to live at ... It isn't there any more. My house was burnt down. And I was badly burnt.
JUDGE	Tell us what happened.

VICTIM	We had a party. Raged on until four a.m. Somebody dropped a cigarette down the back of the sofa. Green vinyl. It smouldered for a while. We didn't notice, we'd had a few drinks and couldn't keep our eyes open. We didn't clear up after the party, and decided to leave it for the morning.
JUDGE	When did you first notice Fire?
VICTIM	Well, the dog started barking. Then I smelled smoke. I got out of bed to have a look, and opened the lounge door. That was a mistake. The handle was hot. When I opened the door, Fire just took off. I never knew flames could be so hot. And there was a funny smell, gas or something from the burning vinyl in the sofa.
JUDGE	What did you do?
VICTIM	Panicked. M'hands were getting burnt. Yelled out for m' wife. Then I tried to open the front door, but it was locked and the key was back on m'bedside table. M'wife grabbed the baby and bundled herself in the doona. She smashed the bedroom window and got out that way.
JUDGE	How did you know that?
VICTIM	I went back for her. But I forgot to shut the doors behind me so the fumes got me. I'm a pretty tall guy and I forgot to crawl down near the floor. You can breathe better there.
JUDGE	Did you call the Fire Brigade?
VICTIM	I think the neighbours did that -
FIRE	*(Interrupting)* About ten minutes later. That's what gave me my chance. If you'd rung straight away, the Fire Brigade would have been there in six minutes.
VICTIM	I didn't know that then.

JUDGE	You were lucky to survive.
VICTIM	My wife survived. I didn't, I died in the fire. I made some stupid mistakes. I should have left the lounge room door shut. I should have rung the fire brigade. If only I hadn't opened the door! I had no fire extinguisher in the house. I'd never worked out beforehand what we should do if there was a fire, because I just didn't think it would happen to us.
FIRE	*(Interrupting)* Then it wasn't all my fault?
VICTIM	The smoke got to us. *(Sitting down, as FIRE USER stands.)*
JUDGE	Next witness, please. This witness will speak in support of the power of Fire.
FIRE USER	My name is ... My job is ... I'd like to defend Fire. They can do some useful things ... *(Actor to fill in gaps.)*
JUDGE	Thank you. Now the next witness. Would the Fire Officer stand please. Tell us some of your experiences with Fire. How do you feel about the danger of Fire?
FIRE OFFICER	My name is ... My job is to ... I respect Fire but I treat them with care because ... *(Actor to fill in gaps.)*
JUDGE	Thank you, Fire Officer. Now a fire-bug has offered to tell a personal story. This child made the mistake of lighting a fire, and the fire spread out of control. The child was badly burnt. Tell us what happened, please, Fire-bug. *(FIRE OFFICER sits as FIRE-BUG stands)*

FIRE-BUG   My name is Smoky Sparks. I am ... years old.
                     I lit a fire ... because ... This was a mistake because
                     ... *(Actor to fill in gaps.)*

JUDGE   We just have time for a word from our Extinguishers.
                     (EXTINGUISHERS stand in turn.)

BLUE EXTINGUISHER
                     I'm blue. I'm filled with foam. Use me on flammable
                     liquids.

RED EXTINGUISHER
                     I'm red. Use me on anything which bums to an
                     ash, but not on flammable liquids or live electrical
                     fires.
                     *(RED WITH BLACK BAND and RED WITH WHITE
                     BAND stand together.)*

RED WITH BLACK BAND
                     I'm filled with carbon dioxide.

RED WITH WHITE BAND
                     And I'm filled with dry chemicals.

RED WITH BLACK BAND and RED WITH WHITE BAND
                     (Speaking in unison.) We're used on live electrical
                     fires or on flammable liquids.

ALL EXTINGUISHERS
                     We do not approve of what Fire does. But if you use
                     us early enough, we can beat Fire.
                     (All EXTINGUISHERS sit.)

JUDGE   Thank you, witnesses. Fire! Do you have any final
                     things to say?

FIRE   Yes, your worship. I am not guilty. I am not to
                     blame. It is what people do with me that matters.
                     I respect drivers who have extinguishers in their
                     cars. I respect parents who have a Fire escape plan.
                     I respect schools who hold regular Fire drills. I stay

	away from ... *(Add examples.)*
	When I get out of control, it is the fault of other people.
	I accuse careless smokers who leave cigarette butts burning.
	I accuse adults who leave matches near young children.
	I accuse businesses whose fire escape doors are blocked.
	I accuse householders who are not prepared,
	(Pointing)
	and I accuse Smoke of being the killer.
JUDGE	I wonder what the jury thinks?
	(Asks JURY.) Discuss it among yourselves.
	What do you think? Guilty or not guilty?
	Hands up those who think Fire is guilty.
	(Pauses)
	Not guilty?
JURY	*(Answers)*
JUDGE	After hearing the evidence and your verdict, I recommend that Fire should be sentenced to be confined. They should be allowed free only when accompanied by a responsible person.
	And at next Monday's session Smoke will be on trial, on a charge of being a danger to our community!
	(A puff of smoke wafts across. Then a fire alarm rings.)

Video and Content Production

Here are some ideas, tips and tricks used to create video, movie and other filmed content.

Stages

There are three stages to the making of a program.
- Planning (Pre-production)
- Shooting (Production)
- Finishing (Post-production)

Don't panic if each takes longer than expected.

Planning (Pre-production)

Before you start 'shooting' (taking the shots with a camera) use this checklist:
- Do you have an adequate budget to make the content?
- Do you have the right equipment? Do you need another camera? light? microphone?
- Visit the place where you'll be shooting (location). Use your eyes as a camera. Think about the position of the sun; it should be behind you when you are shooting. List any unusual shots you might want to take
- Listen. Are there any audio problems? Talk to people who live and work at the location. Are there any noises at particular times of the day or night?
- Will you have enough power? If using batteries, will you be able to recharge them on location?
- Do you have permission to shoot there? Public places such as a railway station or shopping centre are acceptable
- Draw a map to show the crew and the talent how to get there
- Storyboard or 'block' shots before starting.
- Consider the types of shots to be taken at various stages of the play.

Shooting (Production)
- Keep a log (record of shots). This makes shots easier to find when editing. Write down:
  Scene number ...
  Shot number ...
  Take number ...
  Time
  Description of shot
  Comments
- Keep calm. Things often go wrong.

Finishing (Post-production)
This is when the content is edited to make a more effective film, movie or video. Graphics, music and a 'voice-over' may be added.

Content Production Notes

Making a film, movie or video is a team effort. How many people do you have? A crew of four could make the whole clip. The scriptwriter-producer-director could work with the camera-sound-lighting operator, and two actors could be the talent in front of the camera.

But if you have plenty of people to form the crew, who does what?

The **SCRIPTWRITER** creates the idea or concept and writes the script. Choose someone who won't feel upset if the director makes changes to the script. The job may include:
- Writing as part of a scripting team
- Writing several drafts
- Working out a shooting script with the director
- Rewriting on location if the script needs 'fixing up'.

The **PRODUCER** organises the business side of the whole project. You need a person who is a good planner. This job may include:
- Working out how long the content will take to shoot
- Deciding on the final length (in minutes)
- Preparing the budget (and getting the money)

- Selecting the crew
- Choosing and contracting the talent
- Hiring or borrowing equipment
- Handling publicity
- Arranging a 'showing'
- Making sure that everything runs smoothly.

The **DIRECTOR** makes the big artistic decisions. A calm person is needed, someone who is good at getting people to work together. This job may include:
- Choosing and looking after the talent
- Visiting the location to decide on the shots
- Working out the actors' movements (blocking in)
- Deciding how the script is to be interpreted (perhaps drawing a storyboard)
- Not blaming people in public when things go wrong
- Being in charge of the shooting
- Giving certain orders:
  'Stand by to record!'
  'Roll tape!' (Operator then says, 'Tape rolling', and counts to ten before saying 'Speed'.)
  'Action!'
  'Stop Tape!'
- Helping to edit the content; taking credit or blame for the content.

The **ASSISTANT PRODUCER** has to fix up things that may go wrong. Choose someone who is good at taking notes and who doesn't become angry easily. This job may include:
- Preparing a shooting schedule, giving the time, date and place of the shoot (including address and map reference if the location is outside school)
- Preparing a call list of who should be there and what time
- Making notes about props and costumes
- Keeping notes on continuity (so actors look the same in following shots)
- Logging the scenes during shooting
- Doing (almost) anything the producer or director suggests.

The **CAMERA OPERATOR** must use the camera well, but also listen to the director's suggestions. This job may include:
- Checking the equipment before leaving (spare batteries?)
- Hooking up the equipment and the power
- Loading the tape
- Checking the sound for the correct recording level
- Making sure no equipment is damaged or lost.

The **OPERATOR** looks after the filming. When the director says, 'Roll tape!' the operator checks and says, 'Tape rolling', then counts to ten (to leave space for editing, inserting titles etc.) and says, 'Speed'. Then the director says, 'Action!'.

The **AUDIO OPERATOR** records sound during the shoot. This job may include:
- Monitoring (listening carefully to) the sound so that extra noises such as neon lights
- Buzzing are not included
- Recording thirty seconds of 'wild sound' (ordinary noises) which can be used as background if necessary.

The **LIGHTING OPERATOR** puts up or changes the position of lights at the director's suggestion. This job may include:
- Checking and packing all lights before a shoot
- Setting up lights
- Checking and repacking lights.

The **WARDROBE/CONTINUITY** person finds and looks after all the costumes needed. This job may include:
- Reading the cast descriptions to find out what they must look like
- Finding costumes
- Listing what each actor wears
- Checking that actors are wearing the same clothes in different shots
- Packing or returning costumes.

The **PROPERTIES** person finds or makes all the props needed. This job may include:
- Reading the script and listing the props required
- Finding or making the props

- Checking that they are in position
- Making sure that all props are returned.

The **MAKE-UP** person looks after the hair and make-up for all the talent. This job may include:
- Preparing a make-up kit
- Listing the order in which actors are to be made up
- Making-up the talent
- Retouching make-up before a 'take', helping actors to remove make-up, and packing away all cosmetics after the shoot.

The **EDITOR** is the person who rearranges the shots to make the finished content. If the content has been shot to edit (i.e. filmed in the order in which it is to be used), it may not be necessary to use an editing suite.

The **TALENT** means the actors and anybody else in front of the camera, such as an interviewer. They need to sign a 'Talent Release Form'.

The **GOFER** is the person who 'goes for' anything which is needed.

If extra people are available, you may use **FIRST CAMERA ASSISTANT**, **LIGHTING** or **AUDIO OPERATORS**. A **SECOND CAMERA ASSISTANT** could also be chosen.

Checklist: Scriptwriting

Some things to consider when scriptwriting:
- Why are you making this content (for fun, to entertain, or to tell important things)?
- In one sentence, write your main idea
- Is the story worth telling?
- Who might wish to see this?
- Any limits?
  Time? (Must be done within a single lesson? Can only be filmed after school?)
  Budget? (Finance restricted?)
  Equipment? (Too basic for your plans?)
- What research will you need to do?

- What is the best shape for your idea?
  Doco-drama? Drama? Documentary?
- Will you need a narrator or will people speak for themselves?

Sample Storyboard

Story boarding visually outlines scenes and sequences, providing a crucial tool for content makers to plan and communicate their vision effectively. By translating written words into visual representations, story boards streamline the production process for the whole team.

Description	Video	Audio
Toula uses hair-dryer near bathroom basin full of water.		SFX: Hair dryer SFX: Dripping tap Toula: Sings to herself while drying her hair.
Guests arrive for the party.		SFX: Footsteps SFX: Door opening Guest: Chatter about the weather and the food.

Guests are plugging multiple things into an adapter.		SFX: Plugging, rustling. Sarah: Offering to plug in devices into the adpter.
Guests in the kitchen microwaving food.		SFX: Clunk and hum of the microwave. Jane: Turning appliances on and off in the kitchen.

Shot Sizes

Utilising various shot sizes in content production adds depth and nuance to visual storytelling, allowing content makers to control the audience's perspective and emotional engagement. From wide shots that establish context to close-ups that capture intimate details, diverse shot sizes enhance the overall visual impact.

Shot sizes	Example
Long shot or wide shot	
Medium long shot	
Mid shot	

Medium close-up	
Close-up	
Extreme close-up	
Very long shot or extreme wide shot	

82 Workplays by Hazel Edwards

Activities

1. **Storyboarding episodes**
   Following a class discussion on narrative techniques, students collectively watch a selected episode of an emergency services television show. Students are to note camera angles, pacing and character development. In small groups, they can choose to dissert a specific segment of the episode, planning and creating detailed storyboards that encapsulate the storytelling techniques observed.

2. **Different roles**
   After an introduction to the essential functions of paramedics, firefighters and other emergency responders, students are tasked with exploring lesser known yet equally crucial roles, such as emergency dispatchers, search and rescue teams, and disaster management specialists. Using online resources, articles, and potentially even interviews with professionals in the field, students gather information on the responsibilities, skills and challenges associated with these roles. The activity aims to broaden students' perspectives on the multifaceted nature of emergency services careers, encouraging them to appreciate the collaborative efforts involved in ensuring public safety and responding to crises.

Sports Centre

Sports and recreation centres serve as dynamic workplaces that offer diverse career opportunities in the field of sports, fitness and wellness. From management and coaching positions to roles in sports marketing, facility operations and sports therapy, these environments cater to a wide range of interests and skill sets. Careers in sports centres often provide individuals with the chance to engage with a diverse community, promote health and wellbeing, and contribute to the development of athletic talent.

Additionally, working in a sports centre can involve organising events, managing facilities and creating programs that cater to various age groups and fitness levels. With the increasing emphasis on a healthy lifestyle, careers in sports centres not only offer professional growth, but also the satisfaction of contributing to the overall wellbeing of individuals and communities.

How One Group Worked

Choice

After discussion, the group decided to use the sports centre as their setting. A couple of students swam there regularly and felt they wouldn't mind approaching the staff with questions about their jobs.

Visit to Setting

The group agreed that they would visit the sports centre as observer-participants to map out the layout, the look and the dramatic possibilities. 'What ... ?' was the question to keep in mind.

What if someone were drowning in the pool? What would the staff do? What would the other swimmers be likely to do? If a client in the rhythmic gym class pulled a muscle, what would the centre do to help? What were the emergency procedures for heart attack, power failure or fire?

Was the centre busier during certain times of the day? Were there sessions for disabled swimmers or the elderly citizens club?

When did staff change shifts? How long were the shifts?

Were the staff friendly or just polite with the customers? What did they call the users? The public? Clients? Customers? How did staff feel towards the public? Did this show in the way they did their jobs?

Brainstorming Session

The group shared ideas on the possible conflicts which might occur at a sports centre. These might occur between:
a. An instructor and a client who feels he's not getting value for money
b. An attendant and public who use pool as a toilet
c. Staff members over someone not doing their fair share or being late.
d. Perhaps the first aid cupboard was not restocked after use.
e. A member of the public and the cashier, due to complaints about entry prices going up.

Improvisation

The group took job roles and acted out their play.

Other Areas of Interest

Pool regulations
- No running
- No diving into the shallow end
- Use the bathroom not the pool
- No bombing or pushing
- No petting
- No ball games
- No rough play or acrobatics
- No liquor
- No bottles
- Proper swimming attire.

There are lots of signs around a sports centre. One student drew the most common ones to use in the mock up sports centre within the school gymnasium.

Setting

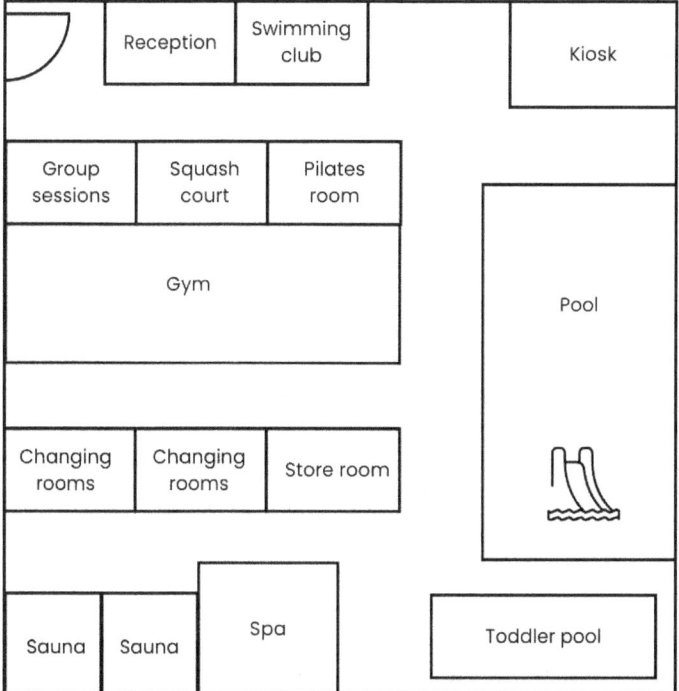

Layout

Visit your local sports or swimming centre.
Map the layout.
Where do the attendants patrol?
What are their instructions?

Interviews

A Day in the Life a Swimming Club Business Manager

Carol has been doing this job for two years. Previously she worked in a recreation centre. She has the necessary qualifications to teach swimming, but that is not essential in her job. She looks very fit.

> *'When I come into work in the morning, I have a general discussion with the co-ordinator of swimming lessons. We talk about how many schools are coming in and whether they need coaches or have their own.*
>
> *Then the co-ordinator spends most of her day beside the pool.*
>
> *I answer phone queries about lessons, water polo or lifesaving, and send out information via email. A lot of time is spent checking stock such as bathers, goggles and water-wings and keeping everything up to date. Basic bookkeeping is needed because I do all the accounts.*
>
> *Public relations is very important in this job, especially being helpful and tactful. When people pay out $50 for a lesson, there's nothing much to show for it. If I'm the last one they speak to before they go home, my manner is very important.*
>
> *3.30 to 6.00 p.m. is our busy time. Parents and children are coming and going every half hour. I'm taking money, getting enrolments and dealing with requests: Sorry Jason can't come Friday. He's got music. Could you change the swimming to 4.30 p.m. Friday night?*
>
> *One of our aims is to help every kid in the district learn to swim. So our phone is manned or the answer phone is used 24 hours a day. Generally, I go home about 6 o'clock except for the two nights*

I work late until about 9 o'clock.

Feedback is important. If people drop out of classes, the coaches are supposed to tactfully find out why. If it's a matter of time or too much travelling that's OK, but if it's something to do with the lesson we want to fix it up immediately. Our coaches are good, but learners are often nervous, whether adults or kids. One mother was so nervous about her son learning to swim that she jumped in fully clothed while he was trying to swim back to the edge. The kid was alright. It was Mum who was worried.

So you have to be a bit of a psychologist when you're dealing with the public.

I like the job. The hours are a bit long, but most people are pleasant, and it's nice when they thank you for something.

Seeing an older person learn to swim is great. It might have been something they've wanted to do for years. When they actually make it to the end of the pool, they're delighted.'

Steve, a Pool Attendant

Morning shift
4.30 a.m.   Get up.
5.30 a.m.   Arrive at work. Check security alarms. Turn on machinery – pumps, filter, lights etc. Check that chlorine level in water is right. Make sure everything is ready and clean. Tidy up change rooms if anything was left from the night before.
6.00 a.m.   Pool opens. Coaches and swimming squads arrive to do their lap work and general training. 'Early bird' regulars swim their laps too.
7.00 a.m.   General cleaning/maintenance – treat tiles with chemicals, replace chipped tiles, clean change rooms thoroughly. Do share of pool duty watching swimmers, usually in one hour bursts of duty because it gets boring just watching and you can go into a trance if you do it too long. Maybe go down the bottom of the pool in scuba gear and clean/replace tiles on the base.

	Handyman work - repair machinery such as the pump, replace light bulbs, solve minor plumbing problems.
9.00 a.m.	Quick coffee break.
9.15 a.m.	Sort out first aid room after dealing with a cut toe. Usually a band aid fixes most of the demands for first aid. But all attendants have lifesaving qualifications and can use oxygen equipment.
10.00 a.m.	More pool patrol. Some 13/14 year olds fooling around. Caution them. Have to haul one out. Move the ropes on the laps lanes to allow more general swimming. Group of fabulous fifties swimmers arrive for their regular date.
11.00 a.m.	Help organise a space for disabled group to have their lunch – with wheelchair access.
12.00 a.m.	Quick lunch break. More pool patrol. Trouble with fuses. Electric clock playing up. Important to fix it because lots of swimmers time their laps.
2.00 a.m.	Finish work.

'One of the best things about the job is the shift work. Seven days on, two days off. Then five on, five off. One week will be early, followed by a late. It does give you time to do other things.'

Pat, a Cashier/Receptionist

'In this job you have to be good at handling people. I take the entrance money, give out locker keys and refunds, sort out lost property and answer any queries.

Take yesterday. A woman rang up complaining about a missing towel which she expected me to go and find immediately.

I had to calm her down and explain that she could have a look through the lost property when she came in. We collect it at the end of each day.

I've been doing this job for fifteen years, so I must like it. I need to know everything about the centre and have a pleasant manner so that people go away happier.'

Activities: Suggested Play Scripts

Script 1

Setting

Sports centre

Cast

- Receptionist/Cashier – takes the entrance money, issues locker keys, looks after lost property and handles bookings for equipment such as water polo balls, kickboards, or scuba diving gear
- Pool attendant – needs to look fit, be fairly big, and have life saving qualifications. Involved with cleaning, so needs to know about chemicals and water testing. Likely to do repair work on the bottom of the pool using scuba-diving equipment, as well as patrols to make sure safety rules are kept. Must know first aid. Wears T-shirt and shorts provided by centre
- Centre manager – responsible for the running of the sports centre. Calls ambulance if anyone is seriously in need of help
- Gym instructor – runs exercise class
- Spa/sauna attendant – keeps sauna at correct heat, cleans inside, checks on users to make sure no-one faints
- Business manager – organises bookings for swimming lessons. Sells bathers, goggles and ear plugs. Organises club activities
- Kiosk organiser – orders and sells food and drinks
- Swimming squad coaches – freelance coaches who organise their own squads of swimmers
- Regulars – swimmers who do laps every day
- Over fifties swimming club (any number).

Problem

Regular swimmers and coaches arrive at pool at 6 a.m. to discover that vandals have wrecked the centre, dropped coloured dye into the pool, left a bad smell in the sauna and mixed up all the sizes in the bathers for sale. Who did it and why?

Script 2

Setting
A learn to exercise to music class in a sports centre which is still being completed.

Cast
- Instructor – who feels nervous because it is his first class. Trying very hard to keep the job and please the clients
- Very fit student
- Worried student who can't touch their toes
- Deaf student
- Carpenter and apprentice – who keep banging nails into the wall as they want to finish their job
- Exercise students – any number.

Problem
Noise. There is so much banging of hammers that the students can't hear the beat of the music. Then something goes wrong with the tape. The students want their money back. How can the instructor solve the problem before the end of the 30-minute class?

Script 3

Setting
Around the pool

Cast
- Pool attendants – any number patrolling
- Swimmers – who are mucking around by jumping on each other
- Girl – being tested for her life saving qualifications
- Tester – who walks beside the pool watching the girl
- Coach
- Swimming squad – at least three swimmers who are being coached.

Problem
While fooling around, someone knocks their head on the side of the pool and goes to the bottom. Attendant notices and dives in. Everyone helps. Meanwhile the power fails and all the lights go out.

Co-op

Co-operative stores and workplaces are rooted in the principles of shared ownership and collaboration. They offer unique career opportunities with a distinct emphasis on community and equitable practices.

Working or volunteering in a co-operative setting allows individuals to actively participate in decision making processes, fostering a sense of ownership and shared responsibility. Many people experience a more inclusive work culture, as co-operatives prioritise fair wages, employee benefits and job security. Additionally, co-operative enterprises frequently contribute to local economic development and sustainability.

Co-operative stores are declining due to the fierce competition from large retail chains and online platforms. Economic pressures, rising operational costs and challenges in adapting to digital advancements further contribute to their diminishing presence.

Play: Help Wanted

Setting
- A shop front which is used as a co-operative workers headquarters

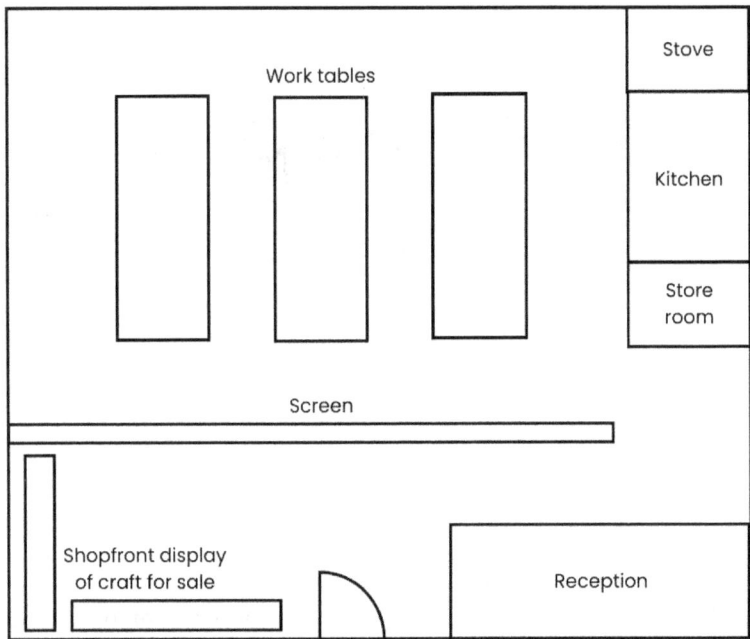

Cast
- Receptionist – answers the phone and helps customers when they first enquire for workers
- Jan – co-op member who cuts lawns
- Customer 1 (Phils) – fussy person who wants lawns cut cheaply
- Customer 2 (Davis) – customer who orders some mugs
- Kay – potter who creates mugs and other ceramics in football club colours
- Ken – co-op member who does the books
- Mrs Manners – customer who needs a babysitter
- Manners children – (3) noisy, nosey, bad mannered children
- Craft workers – any number, making products for sale while waiting for any co-op jobs
- Customers – any number
- Sheep – used as a joke as a lawn mower for a difficult customer.

Props
- Mugs, tools, tables, chairs

Script

RECEPTIONIST	*(On the phone.)* Good morning. This is The Co-op. May I help you?
CUSTOMER PHILS	Yes. I was looking for someone to cut my lawn. Saw your ad in the local paper. It says you go anywhere, do anything. Is that true?
RECEPTIONIST	Almost. I'll just check with our grass cutters. *(Said to the workers.)* Who's available for mowing? *(Several doing craftwork at the back put up their hands and call out.)* No problem. We'll have someone over to you this morning. *(Back on the phone to the customer.)*
CUSTOMER PHILS	What's it going to cost me? When I heard you were a co-op I thought that'd be nice and cheap. How much?
RECEPTIONIST	We charge an hourly rate of $30.00.
CUSTOMER PHILS	That's a lot. You are experienced, I hope. You sound young. *(Receptionist makes a face. Has heard it all before.)*
RECEPTIONIST	How big is your lawn?
CUSTOMER PHILS	Pretty big. Might have trouble finding it under the shrubs and leaves.
RECEPTIONIST	Can you give me your name and address so I can send somebody out there straight away. *(Makes a sign to those working at the table. One girl nods.)*
CUSTOMER PHILS	Do I pay him or you?
RECEPTIONIST	When the job's done, pay her.

CUSTOMER PHILS	It's a girl. To mow my lawn?
RECEPTIONIST	Why not?
CUSTOMER PHILS	How can I be sure she'll do a good job?
RECEPTIONIST	Haven't had many complaints.
CUSTOMER PHILS	Not many. That means somebody has complained. Who was it? What did they complain about?
RECEPTIONIST	It doesn't matter. Jan will be out at your place within the hour. Thank you. I'll just check that address first.
RECEPTIONIST	16 Woods Street.
PHILS	Thank you.
RECEPTIONIST	*(Hangs up as Jan gets tools together.)* You can't please all the people all the time.
JAN	No. Just some of the people, some of the time.
RECEPTIONIST	Coming to the monthly meeting Friday night?
JAN	Yes. Ken should have the accounts ready by then. Last night he was trying to make things balance. Look out. Here comes another customer.
CUSTOMER DAVIS	I'd like to buy a soup mug. One of those in the footy colours. My club is, er, this one here.
RECEPTIONIST	Kay; who makes the pots, does other things in club colours. Ashtrays ...
CUSTOMER DAVIS	I don't smoke.
KAY	*(Coming across to counter.)* Milk jugs.
CUSTOMER DAVIS	I don't drink milk.
KAY	Coffee cups and saucers.
CUSTOMER DAVIS	Don't drink coffee. But I do drink tea.

KAY	You can leave orders. I'll do them especially for you. Even put your name on them if you like?
CUSTOMER DAVIS	*(Whispering)* Would you put ... on them?
KAY	*(Surprised)* I suppose so.
CUSTOMER DAVIS	Thanks. I'll take three. And I'll leave a deposit of $10. Be back next week.
KAY	They'll be ready Monday. *(Customer Davis leaves as Mrs Manners hauls three children into the shop. They touch everything and break a few pieces.)*
MRS MANNERS	I need a babysitter.
RECEPTIONIST	*(Looking at children's mess.)* Yes!
MRS MANNERS	*(Waving a flyer.)* Look at this. It says you'll do anything. Found it in my letter box this morning.
RECEPTIONIST	Almost anything.
MRS MANNERS	Anyway, my children are perfect. You won't have any trouble with them. All my ex-babysitters have said that ... *(Mutters from the worktable.)*
RECEPTIONIST	Excuse me. What is the address?
MRS MANNERS	85 Imerpial Ave. *(Craft workers' groan.)*
RECEPTIONIST	And your name?
MRS MANNERS	Manners. Mrs Manners.
CRAFT WORKERS	*(Behind screen.)* Not Mrs Manners! She's the one with those ... Oh no!
RECEPTIONIST	Thank you Mrs Manners. We'll pick up all the broken artwork. That will have to go on your bill. But we'll also have someone to babysit for you very soon.

Activities

1. **Finish the play.**

    Questions you might try to resolve:
    - Who will babysit for Mrs Manners?
    - What might happen with the Manners children?
    - Who else might become a customer of The Co-op?
    - What other services does The Co-op offer?
    - How might they handle difficult customers?
    - What will they do at the monthly meeting?
    - What type of books must be kept?
    - How do they share the profits?
    - Who might order the sheep as a slow lawn mower?

2. **Co-operative Types Workshop**

    In this activity, students will delve into the co-operative model by researching and presenting findings on various co-operative enterprises. Each group will explore a specific co-operative type, such as worker co-operatives or consumer co-operatives, to understand their organisational structure and community impact. Following their research, students will engage in a mock co-operative meeting, simulating the democratic decision making process. To provide a real-world perspective, a guest speaker from a local co-operative or a visit may be arranged.

Factory, Farm and Railway Station

Delving into careers in a factory, on a farm or at a railway station not only expands students' career horizons but also imparts practical knowledge about industrial, agricultural and transportation sectors.

Discovering roles within a factory introduces students to manufacturing processes, quality control and teamwork, fostering an appreciation for industrial operations. Exploring farm careers offers insights into agriculture, emphasising sustainable practices, crop cultivation, and animal care. Similarly, understanding roles at a railway station illuminates the logistics, maintenance and customer service aspects of the transportation industry.

Suggested Play Scripts

Factory

Setting
The Australian Lolly Company. The production line of a factory which makes a variety of confectionery.

Cast
- Factory hands (any number) wearing uniforms, who:
    - Operate the machines in which sugar, water and other ingredients are mixed to make different kinds of sweets
    - Weigh ingredients before adding them to the pans
    - Set up the moulds to shape the different sweets
    - Clean the machines and pans
    - Check the finished product for imperfections
    - Wrap or pack the sweets before they go to the shops
- Leading hand
- Supervisor/foreman/forewoman
- Shop steward or union representative
- Journalist who's come to write a story on how Easter eggs are made.

Problem
There has been trouble relating to who washes the uniforms which workers must wear while handling food. The company pays an allowance and workers have been doing their own. After a complaint about dirty uniforms from the health department inspector, the company has decided to stop giving workers the allowance and pay a professional laundry to do the job. The factory hands are suspicious that the journalist really wants to write about the uniforms dispute, not about Easter eggs. The factory hands want to keep their uniform allowance.

Additional Conflicts
Machinery is very noisy and dangerous. Perhaps safety guards need to be placed on the machinery to protect the workers?
The fine sugar makes the workplace very dusty. Perhaps a new worker suffers from an allergy.

Farm

Setting
Dairy farm – milking shed

Cast
- Owner – who's thinking of selling the farm.
- Farm labourers (2) – who organise the milking.
- Teenage relative – who's staying for the holidays to see if farming appeals as a possible lifestyle. They are from the city and have never been on a farm before.
- Milk tanker driver. Fond of practical jokes. Quick at the job. Strong views on striking.
- Health department inspector, checking on cleanliness of the property. Very fussy about little details.
- Student from agricultural college on a six week work experience program. Very keen on all the new methods.
- Lots of dairy cows (imaginary or played by students)
- Prospective buyer of the farm, come to have a look around. Suspicious about the reason why the farm is for sale.

Problem
It's been a bad year for the farm, owing to the drought. Because the owner's short of capital and can't get further loans from the bank, the farm must be sold. There has been a strike among the tanker drivers. Need to make property look attractive for possible buyers. Just as the buyer arrives, there is a power failure and the fussy health inspector starts complaining.

Your Play Script
Think of a good opening and a dramatic conclusion to your play.

Make sure that characters have something to 'do' as well as 'say'.

Work out your own play from these dramatic ingredients. Perhaps the characters might decide on their feelings towards each other. What conflicts of ideas or personal values are likely to arise?

Apart from 'milking machines' what props will you need?

Railway Station

Setting
Suburban railway station, with shunting yard.

Cast
- Railway station assistant/porter who
    - Sells tickets to passengers and checks tickets before people get on train
    - Closes platform gates before train leaves
    - Keeps station clean and tidy
    - Answers phone; answers questions about timetables and fares
    - Picks up any mail or parcels left on station
    - Works in parcels office
    - Records movements of trains involved in shunting
- Station master
- Passengers (any number, including frantic parent of lost child)
- Ticket inspectors (2) – checking on passengers
- Lost child
- Railway guard
- Train driver.

Problem
Lots of passengers arrive just before the train. Station master is feeling ill. Child is left on platform when train leaves and parent is carried on to next station. Strange parcel is ticking in the parcels office. Could it be a bomb? What should the porter do? A new all-day travel pass has just been introduced. Passengers are confused.

Your Play Script
Visit your local railway station and watch how passengers behave during peak hours and at quiet times. Talk to the railway staff. Who travels when? How do they feel about wearing uniforms? Are there passengers with unusual requests? Have any incidents occurred which could be used in your play?

Now make up your own group play.

Anywhere

Exploring different workplaces provides students with an opportunity to grapple with real-world issues such as sexual harassment, fraud and ethical dilemmas. This exposure not only equips young individuals with adaptability but also fosters a deeper understanding of the complexities within different sectors. Preparing and understandint there will be some issues not only allows for personal and professional growth, but also instills a sense of responsibility and awareness about the varied challenges that may arise in the dynamic landscape of work.

Play: That's No Job for Them

Setting
- Neutral, so it can be converted from a school to a supermarket and then to an office, factory and hospital.

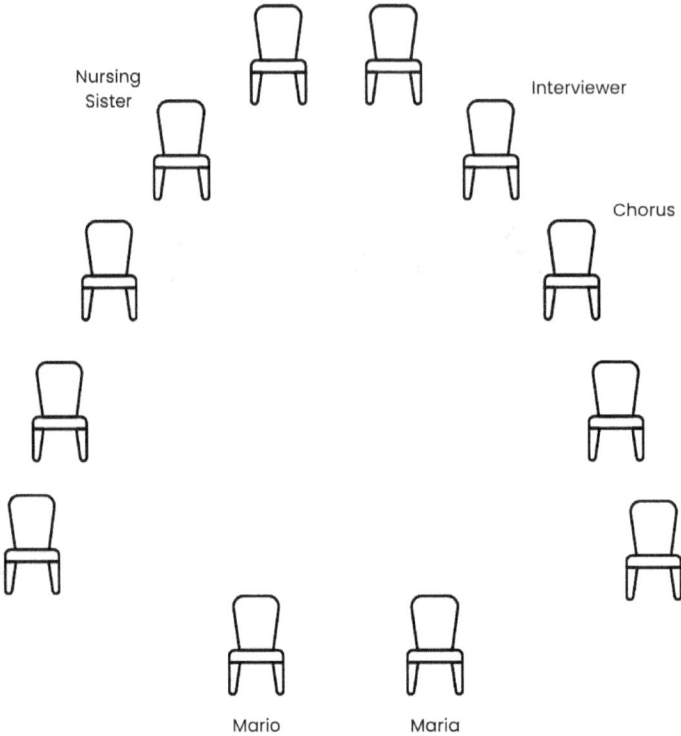

Cast
- Mario
- Maria
- Teachers' chorus (any number)
- Parents' chorus (any number)
- Students' chorus (any number)
- Work chorus (any number)
- Interviewer
- Nurse
- Patient
- It would be possible for the same chorus to play all group roles. The interviewer could also be the patient.

Props
- Sheets of paper
- Supermarket trolleys (perhaps mimed)
- Weight labelled 16 kilos
- White coat for Mario
- Toolbox for Maria
- Bed for patient

Script

Mario and Maria are surrounded by the various choruses which form a semi-circle, stepping forward in turn. All are dressed in jeans and t-shirts, but you can add extras such as glasses for interviewer or teachers. Try to vary the pace at which the choruses speak.

TEACHERS' CHORUS

(Shouting and throwing out sheets of paper to bewildered students who give up trying to read after a while.)
Read this!
Don't do that!
Stand up!
Sit down!
Listen to what I'm saying!
Don't worry about that!
Pay attention!
Stand still!
Hurry up!
Why can't you ....
You'll never finish year 12 ...
What do you think?
Don't you have any ideas?
Be original
Do as you're told
Show some initiative
Think of the group ...
A democratic school like this encourages ...
Don't you ever think ...

STUDENTS *(Including Mario and Maria.)* Yes ...

TEACHERS' CHORUS
Be quiet. Concentrate on your textbook.
Do your exam.
(Parents push supermarket trolleys across stage while chatting. Much slower pace.)

PARENTS' CHORUS What do you think of the school?
Haven't heard anything bad.
What's Maria doing next year?
Might leave school.
Loves little kids. Would make a good mother.
Get a job until she gets married.
What'll she do when the children go to school?
Get a job until she retires.
That's about 35 years. A long time to fill in.

MARIA *(In background.)* 35 years!

PARENTS' CHORUS What's Mario doing next year?
Might leave school.
Trying for an apprenticeship. That's what his Dad always wanted to do.
Is that what Mario wants?
Don't know. Never talk about it. But he's good with his hands.
Like his father.
And kids should do what their parents want.

MARIO *(In background.)* Should they? You can't buy and sell people like supermarket specials.
(Parents' chorus step back into semi-circle.)

STUDENTS' CHORUS
(Stepping forward. Fast paced.)
What subjects are you doing next term Mario?

MARIO Maths, English, Art, PE, Woodwork, Biology.

STUDENTS' CHORUS Good. You'll need your maths for an apprenticeship.

MARIO Maybe. Might do something else.
(Interviewer steps forward, talks to Maria.)

INTERVIEWER Why do you want to be a carpenter?

MARIA Like working with m'hands.

WORK CHORUS We haven't got any suitable toilets.

MARIA *(Smiling)* You've survived so far.

INTERVIEWER Legally, girls can't lift weights of more than 16 kilos.

MARIA Can you?
(Each one of the work chorus lifts weight and hurts back.)

MARIA Lots of older men have back troubles. Perhaps they didn't know how to lift properly or share the load.
(Mario and Maria share lifting the 16 kilogram weight, bending at the knees.)

WORK CHORUS Men's wives wouldn't like it.

MARIA My boyfriend doesn't mind me working with other men. Why should he? Why should they?

WORK CHORUS Carpentry skills are inherited, not learnt.

MARIA *(Smiling)* My grandfather was a carpenter.

WORK CHORUS *(Relieved)* Only inherited from father to son.

MARIA My father was a carpenter too. *(Crosses her fingers behind her back.)*

WORK CHORUS *(Worried)* Perhaps that helps. But ... working outside you'll get sunburnt, overalls aren't very feminine.
(Attempt to put arms around her shoulder; she pushes them away.)

MARIA	Depends on what you mean by feminine.
WORK CHORUS	The men couldn't swear any more.
MARIA	Perhaps I could teach them some new words?
WORK CHORUS	You'll give it up when you get married.
MARIA	Why? It's better paid than being a secretary.
WORK CHORUS	We'll see. *(Work chorus step back into semi-circle. Patient lies down in centre.)*
PATIENT	Nurse. Nurse. Will you change my bed? *(Mario steps out pulling on white coat.)*
PATIENT	Sorry Doctor. I didn't mean you.
MARIO	That's all right. I am the nurse.
PATIENT	But that's women's work.
MARIO	People's work. Now I'll just have to lift you out of bed. The other nurse will help. I don't want to 'do' my back. *(Mario lifts patient, with help of the other nurse.)*
WORK CHORUS	Not many part-time jobs around these days.
PATIENT	Do you get paid the same as the real nurses?
MARIO	*(Grins)* Yes.
PATIENT	Bit of a cissy job isn't it?
MARIO	You're not a cissy and my job is looking after you. *(Leg on bed collapses.)*
PATIENT	The bed leg's gone. Get someone to fix it.
MARIO	The carpenter will fix it. *(Maria walks across stage with her toolbox.)*
PATIENT	She's a female!

MARIO	She can do the job.
PATIENT	All right.
	(Maria fixes bed. Mario fixes patient.)

Activities

1. **The Ending**
   Think of a suitable ending for your version of the play.

2. **Workplace Dynamics Workshop**
   In this interactive workshop, students will delve into common workplace issues, with a particular focus on office politics. Begin by presenting a brief overview of office politics, emphasising its impact on workplace culture and individual wellbeing. Divide the class into small groups and assign each group a specific workplace scenario related to office politics, such as conflicts over credit for ideas, favouritism, or navigating power dynamics. Students will then role-play these scenarios, exploring potential resolutions and strategies to address such issues. Following the role-play, conduct a reflective group discussion where students analyse the observed dynamics and propose effective solutions.

Co-working Spaces

Co-working spaces have grown into dynamic hubs which have changed the traditional concept of the workplace. These shared spaces provide freelancers, entrepreneurs and remote workers with flexibility and shared facilities. They can network, gain a sense of community and learn from others in different industries.

Activities

1. **Virtual Exploration**
   Encourage students to embark on a virtual tour of various co-working spaces, both locally and globally. This activity can involve researching different co-working facilities, exploring their layouts, amenities, and unique features. Students can then conduct a comparative analysis, considering factors such as pricing models, community engagement initiatives and the overall atmosphere of each space. This not only enhances their digital research skills but also provides insights into the diverse approaches that co-working spaces employ to cater to the needs of professionals.

2. **Co-working Quirks**

   In this creative writing activity, students will craft a short play script centered around amusing scenarios in a co-working space. From the classic dilemma of someone pilfering a colleague's sandwich to unexpected situations like shared showers or the introduction of an office dog, students will explore the dynamics of a shared workplace through humour and imagination.

   This challenge encourages students to develop engaging characters, witty dialogue and humorous twists, fostering both creativity and an understanding of the quirks that might arise in collaborative work environments. After completing their play scripts, students can share and perform their creations, turning the classroom into a stage for the comedic nuances of co-working life.

3. **Co-working Space Design Challenge**

   Engage students in a hands-on design challenge where they conceptualise and present their vision for an innovative co-working space. Begin by providing them with insights into the diverse layouts and functionalities of existing co-working spaces. Encourage students to think about the spatial arrangement, technology integration, collaborative zones and aesthetic elements that contribute to a conducive work environment.

   After crafting their designs, students can present their concepts to the class, highlighting the rationale behind their choices. This activity not only taps into their creativity but also hones their presentation skills as they articulate the key features that make their co-working space design unique and effective.

Self Employment

Self employment is increasing. So are freelancing opportunities with flexibility for those with in demand skills. Self employment offers a wealth of benefits, allowing individuals to tailor their careers to their personal needs and family life, and work from virtually anywhere.

Freelancers have the chance to diversify their skill sets, collaborating with diverse clients and gaining exposure to a range of projects. Additionally, self-employment fosters entrepreneurial spirit, as individuals navigate the intricacies of managing their own businesses.

Working from Home

Some self-employed people choose to work from home. Often they call themselves 'freelance'.

The term freelance originally meant a medeival mercenary. Occupations change. Today, the description applies also to the increasing number of highly skilled parents who work from home offices, whilst also caring for young children.

They include accountants, writers, illustrators, solicitors, and fashion designers. A domestic office is financially attractive in terms of low overheads and reduced travelling, but the main advantage is on-the-spot childcare.

'Freelancing from home saves me time, money, and the hassle of getting someone else to pick the kids up from school. I do kindergarten milk and fruit roster in between assignments,' said Mary Frances, a fashion designer.

'The flexibility is invaluable when coping with sick children or in the afternoons when baby has a sleep. It may mean working into the night to finish a project, but at least I have the peace of mind that I'll be there for the kids when they need me,' said Ms Frances.

Critics of home-based freelance work complain that its quality suffers from the interruptions of children. 'Who wants to employ a freelance who has kids screaming in the background when you ring them up?' was one reaction.

Competent freelancers disagree. 'You're only as good as your last piece of work. If that book was botched, you won't get further contracts,' explained Beth, a book designer and mother of two pre-schoolers.

'So don't let kids scribble on pages or mess around when clients call. "Play School" guarantees me one uninterrupted hour of work in the morning. The rest of the time, I just fit around the children's naps or have them minded if I've got a rush job.'

Mary Keenan, a Surrey Hills accountant and tax agent, separates her work into concentrated and 'fiddly'. Delivering material, sorting invoices, or photocopying is 'fiddly' and can be done with the children around. Concentrated work she does between 9.30 am and 3.30 pm in the office attached to her home. An aunt who lives with the family minds Mary's three-year-old daughter when necessary.

Are freelancers mercenary like the medeival ones? 'Until you're established, yes. You do tend to think about money a lot, but most freelancers with young children tend to under charge,' said Vikki Driscoll, a photographer based in Camberwell. 'If you're working on an hourly rate, it's a bit difficult to estimate a fair fee when you've had a lot of interruptions. So you tend to under charge.'

Rae Murphy, a Blackburn computer programmer, disagrees. 'I work on the basis of the normal fee plus a 50% loading to cover holidays and insurance and that sort of thing.

Then I add 50 per cent for my risk factor. Once clients know you are reliable, they are happy to pay. Too many people who work at home get exploited because they need the work badly.

A lot of freelancers get into trouble because they work like mad, but they don't really cost their time properly. At the end of the year, they've worked harder than an employee, but have been paid about a quarter of an employee's wage. That's all right if you love what you are doing, but freelancing can be a hungry business.'

'Once a month I go to a professional practitioners meeting and I subscribe to all the journals in my field' said Mary Keenan, whose tax agency is growing by word of mouth recommendation from clients. 'Sometimes I can do some reading while the children have a swimming lesson on a Saturday.'

Working a seven-day week in concentrated segments is common to freelancers who are also parents. 'I take the kids with me to some clients homes' says Jan, a solicitor from Vermont. 'After all, some of my clients have young children too.'

'Let's be honest,' said Rosalie, a Carlton script writer. 'If you're the mother of young children and you're freelancing from home, you work all the time. I don't know how many hours I spend per week. I just vanish into the study whenever it's possible. If the baby yells, then I leave my computer and go and change the nappy.'

Bob, an illustrator and father of two primary school children, intends to remain a freelance artist. 'If you're highly skilled and build up a good reputation, then you can pick and choose work. That's great. But in the beginning you're just grateful to get any work. Without Anna's income, we would have starved. It took me five years to reach the lowest rung of the income tax form. But my kids and I have a great relationship because I've been around to admire finger painting, put Bandaids on knees and listen to them reading.'

Children don't often appreciate the effort made by a parent who works on a freelance basis. As one four-year-old said, 'My Mummy doesn't go to work. She just draws pictures in the study all day.'

Some self employed people have unusual occupations, which have developed from a hobby or interest into a satisfying business.

Songwriter Harry Nanos developed his musical and lyric writing skills into his 'Singing Portraits' business. He composes lyrics and music for birthdays, anniversaries, weddings, football club celebrations and even love affairs.

'I enjoy the challenge of writing something different each time' says 26-year-old Harry.

Before he can compose a special song, Harry requires certain information: 'The person's name and interests. Whether it's to be funny or serious. How old they are. Something about the person who is ordering the song and why it is being given.

Just in case of any slips, Harry always checks, by reading the lyrics back before finally recording. Considering the time taken to write and record, Harry's fee for 'the lot' which includes a high quality recording is not high.

He wrote a new football club song for Yarraville. They were holding a special celebration and players couldn't remember the words of the old club song. So Harry was commissioned to write a new one.

Some of the song titles give an idea of the contents. 'Yes, Megan's Getting Married Today' is one. A father commissioned a song for his six-year-old's birthday. A best man ordered a song for the bride and groom.

At present Harry averages four songs a week, but he would like to expand his business and also write for advertising agencies.

Recently, an American poet began a brisk business in personalised poems for special occasions, written on parchment and framed. Harry Nanos's 'Singing Portraits' are filling a similar need.

Activities

1. **Radio program**

    You are responsible for producing a radio interview program called Workers Half Hour.

    Today you will interview three people who work for themselves. Prepare the questions to ask them. The questions below will give you a start.
    - Why do you work for yourself?
    - How do you decide when you've done enough?
    - What would you do on an average day?
    - Do you earn as much as a person working for a big company?
    - Do you work from home? Why?
    - What would you like to change about your work style?

    Some suggested occupations for the interviews:
    - Cartoonist
    - House cleaner
    - Gardener
    - Handyperson
    - Farmer
    - Hobby sheep shearer.

    Now make a recording and play it through the school loud speaker system.

2. **Business Podcast Launch Challenge**

   Many self employed people and freelancers rely on podcasts to talk about their business. In this activity, students will embark on the exciting journey of creating and launching a podcast for a chosen business. Over several sessions, they will plan and develop engaging content, explore recording and editing techniques, design branding elements, and formulate a marketing strategy for the launch.

   This immersive project not only introduces students to the world of podcasting but also hones their skills in content creation, storytelling, branding and marketing. The culminating step involves the launch of the podcast, providing students with valuable insights into the dynamics of promoting a business through this contemporary and influential medium.

Exploring Job Considerations

Starting a career journey is more than choosing a job title. Consider if you like that type of work environment and want to become skilled in that field and which qualifications are needed. Questions include supervision preferences, team work, machinery operation and educational prerequisites. Finding the answers mean individuals can make informed decisions for careers long term.

Some issues to consider when finding out about a job:
- What are the specific roles and responsibilities associated with the job?
- Will you work under supervision or alone? Which do you prefer? Why? Would it give you more confidence to be supervised at the beginning?
- Are you likely to be part of a team? What will your contribution be?
- Is there any special machinery involved? If so, how and when will you learn to operate it?
- What level of education is needed?
- Are certain subjects required?

- Is the job mainly outdoors or inside? Any shift work involved? Overtime? Is there any heavy physical work? Will you be offered any opportunity to travel?
- Where is the job located? What is the expected commute or how will you get there?
- What is the starting wage or salary? Any chance of a bonus? Is overtime paid? Any allowance for clothing or tools?
- Is the training 'on the job' or will you need to go to school part-time? Any night classes needed?
- What are the legal requirements of starting a new job? What's the superannuation scheme? Workers compensation?
- Any additional benefits offered?
- How does the company prioritise work-life balance?
- What opportunities exist for career growth and development?
- Can you take time off to study? Any help with fees?
- Are you likely to get a promotion? Do you need special qualifications to be promoted?
- How would you describe the company's culture and values?
- Is your job likely to be superseded by a robot or AI?
- Is this field of employment likely to expand or cease to exist?

www.ingramcontent.com/pod-product-compliance
Lightning Source LLC
Chambersburg PA
CBHW052151110526
44591CB00012B/1937